DANCING DAUGHTER

SUSAN LAMBERT

SL PUBLISHING

SL Publishing

PO Box 1194, Kingscliff NSW 2487, Australia

susanlambert.com.au

Published April 2019.

Copyright © Susan Lambert 2019.

This book is copyright. Apart from fair dealing for the purposes of private study, research, criticism and review as permitted under the Copyright Act, no part of this book may be reproduced by any process without the express permission of the publisher.

ISBN

Paperback: 978-0-6485174-0-5

Ebook: 978-0-6485174-1-2

Scripture quotations marked TPT are from The Passion Translation®. Copyright © 2017, 2018 by Passion & Fire Ministries, Inc. Used by permission. All rights reserved. ThePassionTranslation.com.

Scripture quotations marked NASB are taken from the New American Standard Bible® (NASB), Copyright © 1960, 1962, 1963, 1968, 1971, 1972, 1973, 1975, 1977, 1995 by The Lockman Foundation. Used by permission. www.Lockman.org

Managing editor: Belinda Pollard

Cover designer and illustrator: Eli Walker

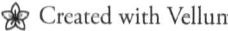 Created with Vellum

*To my mother,
who loved with strength, courage and grace.
I am forever grateful.*

*To my father,
forgiven and loved.*

*To my husband Greg,
who has always loved me unconditionally.
Forever us.*

*To my sons Jake and Clayton,
to be your mother has been the greatest privilege and
blessing of my life.*

CONTENTS

Preface	vii
1. Dancing Daughter	1
2. Miracle in the Mayhem	3
3. Silent Melody	10
4. Butcher to Bartender	18
5. Child Soldiers	26
6. Broken Fences	32
7. For Better or for Worse	43
8. The Family Anthem	58
9. Seaside Sojourns	63
10. Life and Loss	70
11. Teenage Bliss	80
12. Changing of the Guard	91
13. Derailed	99
14. Rogue Waves	117
15. The Letter	122
16. A New Dance	126
Photographs	133
About the Author	139
Domestic and family violence support services, Australia	140

PREFACE

THE WALKING WOUNDED

This is a cautionary tale for all those who have grown up amongst the rigours of domestic violence or trauma as a young child. This story is not a vengeful return to the past to cast blame, nor is it a self-indulgent sojourn to garner sympathy. Rather, it is the reconciling between a wounded child and an adult self, seeking wholeness.

It is ultimately a story of hope, healing and renewal.

This story goes well beyond the childhood scars of trauma and encourages us to walk a path for our life that is not shaped by past wounds.

We need the knowledge to recognise and confront the discordant childhood melody that may persist, playing subtle, malevolent notes in the background of our lives.

For this recognition ultimately holds the key to our healing. It is not a dismissal of trauma, nor is it a denial of our pain. Our scars, once healed, will become the fabric of who we are.

Danger lurks when we don't realise there is a discordant childhood melody playing at all, or, more gravely, we are unwilling to confront our past to move into an abundant, whole future.

If we leave our wounds open and bleeding, they may continue to silently ooze more pain and grief into our future.

It takes much bravery to return to a battlefield once the war is over. There are casualties after a war. And yet, the beginning of our freedom can be found there.

I went back to the battlefield of my childhood initially for my own personal healing. It was only as I stood in the desolate remains of my own memories that I realised there was another reason far beyond myself.

I was not alone. I saw others, stumbling about, wounded and aimless.

My story is a call to all those who may also see themselves as the walking wounded. Those who instinctively know they need to bravely return to their own childhood battlefield, to confront their pain, lay down their weapons and find peace and hope for a better future.

SUSAN LAMBERT

DANCING DAUGHTER

My lower back ached as I desperately stood on my tiptoes, trying to be tall enough to dance with him. I was seven years old. I held my body as straight as I could, frantically counting dance steps in my head, to hold the correct waltz rhythm, to keep him happy. The sleep-out—a closed-in back veranda of our home—created the perfect makeshift dance floor, with its long, rectangular shape and smooth, brown, linoleum floor. Glass louvres ran along the back wall, always slightly ajar to catch any semblance of breeze. The bottle green vinyl lounge with small black buttons, some missing, never functioned properly as a seat due to the mountain of clothes piled high.

"Keep your head up!" he yelled.

Whiskey and perspiration reeked from his clothes as he pulled me closer. He was still wearing his black work trousers and shoes, although he had removed his shirt to escape the heat, leaving just a white singlet.

His short black hair looked greasy from copious amounts of Brylcreem. His olive-skinned face glistened with an alcohol-fuelled glow. He was not an overly tall man and yet had strong arms built from years working as a butcher. My father's dark brown eyes, however, were by far his most striking physical feature. Remarkably, they still sparkled through the glazed dullness of addiction.

The old vinyl record player crackled, its needle jumping in well-worn scratches. Old-time waltz songs rang out from the player and the sweet melody of the music seemed to mock the true reality of the dance. At times, I reluctantly looked up into his grimacing face, which seemed to hold a mix of anger, love and torment.

My mother appeared at the door, with that ever-familiar desperately sad face. She begged my father to turn the music off, so I could go to bed. "It's late and it's a school night," she pleaded gently, trying to reason with his intoxicated, irrational brain, but he was completely adrift in a drunken haze.

"Piss off! I'm teachin' my daughter to ballroom dance!" He dismissed her with an aggressive wave of his hand and I inwardly panicked, thinking she may have triggered another physical outburst from him.

I tried to reassure her it was fine, using just my eyes—an unspoken language of survival that had evolved between us.

This dance, which had begun many hours ago, was not a special father–daughter childhood moment etched in time—rather, it was a dance of desperation.

It was a dance to save my mother.

MIRACLE IN THE MAYHEM

On a hot, dry January afternoon in the year of 1980, my deliverance arrived in the form of an official-looking letter with a government stamp on the front. It had been left poking awkwardly out of our small, paint-peeled tin letterbox, and I knew the contents had the potential to change my life.

Amongst the chaos of our family life I had somehow managed to gain successful entry to university! The elation was short-lived.

I recall the hushed conversation between my mother and the uncle who had come to deliver the bad news, before my father arrived home drunk and indignant about his supposed unfair dismissal. He had been caught drinking on the job.

Impeccable timing, as usual.

My father had of course been caught numerous times and given many warnings, but all had gone unheeded. I heard desperate weeping as my mother stood on the front footpath with her head in her hands. The family was now without an income apart from her motel-cleaning wage. My uncle stood awkwardly with his hand on her shoulder, trying to comfort her. A meagre cleaner's wage was barely going to cover the bills, let alone support my dream of going to university.

"Susan, can you come into the lounge room please?" said my mother.

The lounge room was always reserved for serious conversation and I knew what she was going to say before she had spoken a word, so I rudely interrupted her.

"I know, I get it. I can't go to university because we can't afford it." My tone was aggressive and full of anger.

My mother dissolved in tears and for the first time ever I didn't feel sorry for her. I felt sorry for me.

"Sweetheart, I'm so, so sorry," she said.

"Yeah, I know you are." I headed for my bedroom, where I slammed the door behind me and threw myself dramatically on my bed.

I cried silently into my pillow. Of all the pain my father had inflicted upon our family over the years, this was probably the worst of all. His addiction was now spewing implications for me way beyond the walls of our home. My father may have been trapped, but I sure as hell was not staying inside those prison walls, he had forged for himself.

A FULLY-FUNDED SCHOLARSHIP TO attend university

was my only possible escape. I was unsuccessful in the first round offers and my prospects looked grim.

My grandmother was living with us, recovering from an illness. One afternoon, I sat on the edge of her bed and shared my desperation. Mardi, as we affectionately called her, was a woman of few words. When she spoke, we listened intently, for her hard life was in itself a glowing portrayal of wisdom.

"I am going to pray and you will go to university," she said as she reached across and took my hand in hers. Her hand felt warm and wrinkled, yet still strong regardless of her age. She prayed aloud with a quiet, composed, unwavering faith that seemed to reach my innermost core.

"Man plans, God commands" was the biblical mantra she had adhered to for most of her life.

I was drawn to her faith.

It gave me a sense that regardless of seemingly insurmountable circumstances, life was fluid and things could change. Fate and destiny were not set in stone in my grandmother's world, for she had seen the power of faith in her own life. To be honest, I wasn't sure about a God who could remain silent in the face of my childhood terror. But I desperately wanted to escape, and if that was on the back of my grandmother's faith-filled prayer, well, unashamedly, I was in.

APART FROM MY MOTHER, my grandmother was the strongest woman I had known. She had developed a steely determination originating in a very sad and traumatic childhood.

In the early 1900s, Dorothy was only ten years old when her parents both tragically died within months of each other, from diseases that are no doubt preventable now. Her father was a boundary rider on a nearby sheep station where his duties involved riding the outer perimeter, to check the condition of the fences and collect any stock that may have gone astray. From all accounts, one afternoon he was struck down with excruciating pain and bundled into the back of a horse and cart to be transported from Temora, a small town some six hours south-west of Sydney, to the nearest hospital in Goulburn. Sadly, his life ended in the back of that horse and cart during that painful, jolting journey, succumbing to complications from gallstones. Her mother was apparently grief stricken and died some months later from unknown causes, leaving Dorothy and her sisters orphaned. As was often customary in the harshness of that era, the children were ushered to a nearby farmer's barn where local families would gather to decide the plight of the forlorn young orphans.

Most families were impoverished themselves and struggling to meet the needs of their own. This meant keeping the children together was not possible. And so, it followed that they were separated and adopted by four different families. My grandmother was sent to live in Sydney, with a lady known only as Aunt Doll, a friend of the family. She owned a milliner's shop and my grandmother earned her keep by maintaining a clean house and babysitting Aunt Doll's children.

In Dorothy's early twenties, this arrangement came to an abrupt end, for no apparent reason—although it was rumoured that my grandmother was ordered from the home after helping Aunt Doll's young daughter, who had found herself pregnant and in desperate need of help. If this was the true catalyst for sending my grandmother away, it would have been the second time grief and abandonment visited her life. Whilst I cannot begin to fully understand how sadness would have impacted my grandmother, it does tell me much about the woman who raised my mother.

DOROTHY LEFT Sydney and returned to the small town of Temora where she had lived as a young girl. Alone, with little money and still unaware of where her siblings were, it was not surprising that in Temora, Dorothy met and soon married a young man called Jack. It was also in Temora that my mother was born, followed closely by her brother. The family then moved several hundred miles to the central western plains to Dubbo to make their home.

Many years later, my mother, sorting through my grandmother's personal belongings, would accidentally discover perhaps part of the reason for the hasty move. An old rusty biscuit tin hidden in the back of my grandmother's wardrobe held a secret for some sixty years. Inside that tin was my mother's birth certificate and grandparents' marriage certificate rolled up in brown paper and bound together by a frayed black silk ribbon.

My mother's birth date was less than nine months after the marriage, which meant she had been conceived out of wedlock. Today, this would be of little social consequence, and yet in the early 1900s being born out of wedlock brought shame upon a family. Perhaps more unjustified shame settled upon my mother that day, when she discovered the documents so secretly hidden. I recall her weeping as she looked at the documents and then folded them quickly and placed them back in that old tin. I can't be sure why she was overcome by grief at this discovery, although it may have served to confirm a belief of unworthiness that had slowly devoured her self-confidence during the loveless marriage she had endured.

But I have leapt forward again.

Dorothy set about building her own family in Dubbo and the years that followed saw the birth of two more children—identical twin girls, born in the front bedroom of her home. My grandmother had no doubt created what she must have longed for through those lonely childhood years in Sydney: a family of her own.

She guarded it with a fierce protectiveness.

I HELD the scholarship application letter in my hand, summoning up the fortitude to open it. My mother sat opposite me at our faithful kitchen table that had weathered a lifetime of contrasting scenes—both love and violence. Deep lines traversed her forehead as though ants had burrowed tunnels in her weathered skin. Her blue eyes had long lost their shine. Her face was flushed due to the extra weight she had gathered over the years as a protective emotional shield.

I caressed the envelope, hoping a slow, tender approach might somehow influence the news inside. I broke the seal and unfolded the letter, our combined sighs the only noise in the kitchen. I reached across for her hand, looked down and began to read aloud.

"Dear Susan,
   It is with much pleasure that we inform you that your application for a teaching scholarship has been successful—"

My mother leapt to her feet, screaming, crying and clapping her hands above her head, before I could finish the first paragraph. Her loose arm skin wobbled wildly as she raised her hands and punched the air like a boxer who had delivered a knockout blow in the final round. Her short physical stature had never reflected her true inner strength.

I jumped up and joined her in a victory dance, right there in the middle of our old familiar kitchen. My mother's determination to free her children had become more resolute with each passing year. I had a deep sense that, by gaining an education, I would be handing her one of the few triumphs she would experience in her life.

She deserved a triumph.

SILENT MELODY

J glanced around my bedroom for the last time and shed no sentimental tears birthed from fond family memories. It wasn't that there were no moments of joy to recall, rather, that they had been submerged beneath the turbulence that was my childhood. I didn't feel any deep connection to the house I grew up in. The violent family battles that had played out there stole any sense of sanctuary a child might usually feel.

My mother stood stoically on the red concrete veranda at the front of our home with her head held high, waiting for our final embrace. Her rounded frame was hidden beneath one of the many oversized, flowing kaftan dresses she had sewn herself. Her hair was now turning a white-silver shade of grey, with only traces of the auburn that had once adorned her. This woman, who had been a victim of domestic violence for most of her married life, had secured a victory through her youngest daughter. I was heading to university and breaking the cycle. It was our miracle in the mayhem.

We shared a long, desperate hug and it was only then that my tears flowed—for a mother who despite the traumatic circumstances she found herself in had loved her children beyond herself.

I naively thought I was leaving the scarred remains of my childhood behind in that old weatherboard house that morning, like the first chapter of a story that had already been told. I was yet to understand that the silent scars of domestic violence or trauma can shadow a child. A relentless song of shame and humiliation can accompany a person, like a drawn-out symphony for years to come. This discordant refrain would whisper the softest of notes that at first I could not hear.

A silent, dangerous melody.

As my life unfolded, I would be challenged time and time again to find the courage to change the notes of that malevolent melody and write a new composition of my own.

My mother was the eldest daughter. She had adopted all the characteristics that accompanied her birth order. Responsible, mature and the caretaker of her younger twin sisters, she developed qualities that would serve her well in the hard times that were to follow. As my own life has unfolded, I have become increasingly convinced that not knowing the twists and turns our life may take, nor the joys or sorrows that may lie ahead, is a compassionate gift to us, lest we lose hope. The far horizon continually beckons us, calling us forth to kinder days.

My mother's generation grew up against the backdrop of World War II and the economic depression that followed. My parents' stories of bomb shelters, food stamps, and blackouts at night huddled around a transistor radio on the kitchen table were so foreign to me. Their stories gave me a glimpse into a childhood so different to mine and yet the same in so many ways. Their childhood and mine were shaped by trauma, just of a different kind.

My mother was raised with a strong sense of family, hard work, determination and an unshakeable faith in God. This was a generation that didn't complain readily and adopted a suffer-in-silence attitude to life. While this might sound admirable, this hard approach left little room for my mother later, to find help when she needed it most.

My mother met and married my father in 1948. I find it incredible that, at the time, my father didn't drink alcohol. From all accounts, he was the life of the party due to his outgoing personality and clever humour. This conflicts somewhat with the theory that women knowingly choose an alcoholic as a partner. Regardless of the accuracy of the theory, I have always found this perception shifts the blame unfairly, as it casts a shadow of accusation over the victim.

In hindsight, I am now convinced my mother quietly carried much of the guilt about our home life, and the unspoken inference that perhaps she had brought it all on herself. Yet, this was the 1950s and women had little independence and few choices. My mother had to cease work as a dressmaker once she was a married woman due to the "marriage bar", a social policy that existed in the 1950s and early 1960s. As a newly married woman, my mother was now indeed at the financial mercy of her husband. The stage was set.

I ARRIVED at university late one Sunday afternoon and followed the signs to B Block, an ageing, red brick, two-storey building which would become my home for the next three years. I pushed open the heavy front doors and dragged my suitcase up two flights of concrete stairs to my dormitory room. I kept my head down because I felt like an impostor. When secrecy and shame have been hallmarks of your childhood it leaves an odd feeling of being misplaced—that you don't belong. I leaned tentatively against the door of my room and was happy to scurry inside and gather myself. A dusty smell greeted me. I felt tears swell in my eyes as the realisation I was all alone struck unexpectedly. Homesickness was not something I had expected to encounter, and yet I should have realised that a childhood spent keeping my mother safe was bound to create strong bonds.

The room was sparsely furnished with a single bed in one corner, a timber desk in the other and drab, dark blue curtains hanging limply on the windows. The small size of my room and the tired décor meant little to me as I sat on the bed and perused my new home. This dated, rectangular, slightly claustrophobic space felt strangely liberating.

For the first time, I sensed a feeling of excitement at the prospect of a future.

I can't recall ever really thinking about a future, as a child. Perhaps the intensity of the now did not allow me the luxury of dreaming what I might be in the world. My childhood had been mostly spent in survival mode. I had not been afforded the luxury of developing any deep longings or passions to guide my life. So it was that I stumbled into a teacher's degree, after a very clever marketing video of rolling green hills on the south west slopes of New South Wales was played at my high school during a careers information night.

Riverina College was located in lush green country, which appealed to me after a childhood of the muted yellow tones of wheat and parched grass and the rolling red dust storms. The contrast between the dry western plains and the green fertile hills of the Riverina region seemed to hold a sense of hope and renewal. A renewal I was unaware I needed at this naïve stage of my life.

I had been drawn to the original homeland of the Wiradjuri people, one of many indigenous communities that had lived on the Hay Plain and surrounding rivers. European settlement in the 1830s had disrupted traditional practices. The women of the Wiradjuri communities had been displaced and some forced to work as domestic slaves, many losing their identity.

I arrived with so much more than those indigenous women who had gone before me, and yet my identity had also been damaged. Regardless of what had drawn me to this university, I was oblivious to the shackles of fear and anxiety that had imperceptibly attached themselves to me as a child. I was even more unaware of their ability to ensnare my steps and cause me to stumble. If only someone had warned my young self: beware of the trauma you have seen, for it may guide you down paths that will continue to erode your self-worth and identity.

It is here where my story must once again return to my childhood.

I have come to learn that finding the courage to return to our battlefields, whatever they may look like for each of us, is in fact the only way forward. Real authentic pursuit of wholeness involves looking squarely at your life in the present through the lens of your past. Some adhere to the notion of never looking back, lest one becomes trapped in the pain, never to return. I personally have found this notion to be unhelpful.

Your past matters.

Your past informs your present.

MY FAMILY HOME was a small weatherboard house with a tin roof, typical of the 1950s, in a small country town on the central western plains of New South Wales, Australia. That old tin roof ironically created some of the few happy memories I have. The sound of the heavy rain pelting on that tin roof was both deafening and exhilarating at the same time. I remember sitting with my mother on the back veranda "storm watching" as we fondly called it. The scent of the storm always preceded its actual arrival with its sweet, pungent, earthy aroma. The rumbling of distant thunder only served to add to the excitement as we huddled together. The finale was always the eventual downpour of rain thrumming on our tin roof.

I was the youngest of three children and I shared a bedroom with my sister, while my eldest brother had the luxury of his own room, albeit a small side section on the back veranda, known as the sleep-out. We had a huge extended family with an array of aunts, uncles, grandparents and cousins all living nearby—or "within spitting distance" as my father would so eloquently express.

We celebrated everything together—birthdays, wedding anniversaries, Easter and Christmas. My family loved a party, and those gatherings would become some of the happiest memories of my childhood. On reflection, the love shared amongst my extended family probably saved us all emotionally, at times when my mother was barely hanging on.

How my father changed from a non-drinking husband and father to a violent alcoholic is not something I fully understand. He was the youngest of nine children born to a father who was a hardworking blacksmith. I don't have a full knowledge of my father's childhood apart from the fact that the family struggled financially and he was not overly loved. My father was forced to leave school at fifteen years old to work in his father's blacksmith shop to help support the family. This was not uncommon.

The most significant event would be his conscription into the army at eighteen and his service in Tarakan, Indonesia. It was common for soldiers to smoke and drink alcohol while at war and yet my father returned and did not continue with any of these habits at that time. The unspoken trauma of war upon those young men, and their silent struggle to find peace, has since been well documented and more fully understood. Post war, many soldiers arrived home with little support to assist with their transition back into normal life. I suspect our family was one of many to suffer the ongoing emotional scars of war, as those young men unknowingly carried their burdens into marriage and parenthood. I will never know for sure if his time at war was a catalyst for his alcohol addiction. Perhaps the default position of drinking alcohol had been locked into gear as a young soldier on high alert. Either way, this knowledge does little to dull the pain of the trauma unleashed upon our family.

My father met and married my mother, bought a butcher shop and their life together began, full of promise.

BUTCHER TO BARTENDER

I snuggled down in my bed, feeling warm and cosy under a heavy woollen blanket. The wind and rain howled outside, wrapping itself around the weatherboard walls of our home, making the wooden window frames in my bedroom rattle in violent, intermittent bursts. Winter in Dubbo was always bitterly cold and I longed to drift off into a deep, blissful sleep and yet a familiar anxiety slowly crept through my body as I waited. The warmth from the electric blanket teased me, trying to lure me into an abandoned slumber. That was barely an option: I had to be awake and alert.

Perpetually on duty.

The shrill ring of the phone pierced the stillness of the night. I heard my mother run to pick up the phone in an effort not to wake her sleeping children. I immediately sat up, poised, as my father's loud, abusive voice echoed beyond the earpiece and found its way into my bedroom. I threw back the bed covers and quickly dressed, pulling on my fleecy green tracksuit. I was standing beside my mother in minutes.

"I'm coming with you," I declared, and she knew from past experience that to argue with me was fruitless.

My father had finished his night shift at the bowling club where he worked and had demanded a ride home. I climbed into the front seat, as I knew this forced him to sit in the back of the car, keeping a safer distance between him and my mother. It was freezing, though thankfully the rain had eased, and my mother pulled her oversized woollen cardigan tightly around her shoulders and shivered. I found myself staring at her cardigan, suddenly realising how old and misshapen it looked. The buttons were all different sizes and it had numerous pulled threads. I had the odd thought that they looked like dead worms. I suddenly wanted to buy her a new one.

My attention was drawn back by the crunching sound of ice on the windscreen as my mother tried to wipe it clear with an old wet towel. I was scared, partly because the night was pitch black and partly because I knew what awaited us. I started rehearsing the scenario in my mind, conjuring up distracting responses that would keep my father calm. There was little conversation on the way and as we arrived at the club, I begged my mother not to argue back with him. "Just keep the peace" had become my desperate childhood mantra.

"Don't worry if he swears, cause I'll block my ears," I reassured her.

My mother reverse-parked the car out the front of the bowls club under the weathered kurrajong trees. The roots of the trees had long rebelled against the bitumen road and pushed their way up to make uneven mounds. The car bounced as we reversed and the wheels contended with the uprisen roots, and we suddenly came to a lurching stop as my mother hit the brake pedal way too hard. Her driving skills had always lacked confidence. She reached down under the steering wheel and, using both hands, wrestled with the park brake to pull it out and secure the car.

Now, we waited. He always made us wait. I assumed he was throwing back a couple of quick shots of whisky to fortify himself for the drive home. The wait was almost more frightening than the reality. My mother started a game of I-spy in an attempt to distract me and I played along, trying to pretend I was coping. Always pretending.

"I-spy with my little eye, something beginning with S," she whispered, her tired voice masked by fake animation.

Deep inside, fear consumed me. The folly of I-spy seemed so ridiculous in comparison to surviving the car ride home.

"Star," I called, just to keep up the pretence.

My mother started clapping at my answer. "Well done, darling. So clever!" Her exaggerated happy-voice annoyed me now.

Our game was abruptly interrupted by the sound of the back door being ripped open and slammed with such frightening force it shook the old Holden Premier to its core. It's not surprising I am still startled by loud, unexpected noises to this day. My mother pulled slowly away from the curb and we began our car journey home.

He was in fine form tonight. He started yelling and punching the back of my mother's red vinyl seat before we had even reached the first corner. She leaned forward over the steering wheel to protect herself. I wasted no time and launched into action, utilising all of my well-rehearsed distraction skills. I prattled on nervously about school and hockey practice and this calmed him momentarily, until we passed the old sandstone church, a landmark that announced we were about halfway home. He was restless and writhed around in the back seat, crossing and uncrossing his legs, trying to dispel some of his unspent rage. It was as though the alcohol was pulsing through his body like some alien force he had no control over.

My mind raced with options to dispel his anger. "How was work today?"

In my desperate search for the right words I soon realised I had chosen the wrong ones, as he exploded into his all-too-familiar litany of accusations.

"Ask your bloody mother how work was. I get no damn thanks for nothin' around here." Then suddenly, like a wild animal that had finally broken free from a cage, he yelled with such intensity that the veins on his neck swelled purple, and his brown eyes almost bulged beyond their sockets.

"You are such a bitch of a woman, turning the whole family against me," he screamed, punching the back of her car seat again just for good measure, in case she hadn't felt it the first time.

"Kevin, please don't," my mother screamed in anger, her vow of silence made to me earlier now broken, worn down by his continual vitriolic abuse.

I swung around in my seat and was greeted by pulsating neck veins and a horridly distorted face.

Such unadulterated rage is hard for a young child to look at directly, so I squinted my eyes a little to dim my view. As I looked at the grotesque image that was my father's face, a deep, guilt-ridden, childish secret surfaced.

I wished he would die.

Right there, in the back seat of our family car.

I DESPISED where my father worked. It wasn't exactly a fancy occupation working behind a bar, although he did have the title of "bar manager" on his badge, which lifted his social standing a little. I always said the word "manager" loudly and dropped "bar" completely, or mumbled it, especially when I was talking to my friends at school about my father's occupation.

He wasn't meant to end up there. He started his married life working in his own butcher shop, just down the road from where we lived. My mother did the bookkeeping while my father dealt with the meat and charmed the customers with his humour and outgoing personality. The meat was housed in a cold room with very low temperatures, and over a period of years the extreme temperatures started to take their toll on his health.

Repeated lung infections followed, and the doctor advised my father to sell the butcher shop. This must have been a very difficult decision, since all my father had known was butchering. I suspect he must have shouldered some guilt about having to let the shop go. I suspect this was the first major emotional upheaval to confront my father since his return from the war. The first trigger perhaps. I vaguely remember as a young girl inadvertently walking in on my parents' conversation about future job prospects one afternoon.

My mother was peeling potatoes in the kitchen sink. Potatoes often featured in our meals, no doubt a cheap option for a lot of families in the 1960s.

"They said they'll train me up," he insisted, but my mother looked troubled and I could tell she wasn't convinced, by the frown that had gathered on her forehead.

"Well I gotta earn a quid doing something," said Dad.

It had been a few months of very little money coming in, and I could sense my mother's concern, hidden in her deep sigh and by the way she haphazardly tossed the potatoes into the boiling water on the stove beside her.

"I'll just do it part time, like, till somethin' else comes up," he suggested, and this seemed to convince my mother a little more.

I watched as she flicked the tea towel over her shoulder. As kids, we knew this gesture by our mother meant she was reaching her overwhelmed stage. While my mum was distracted by the conversation with my father, the potatoes suddenly erupted and boiling water billowed from the saucepan, like lava. A burnt smell filled the kitchen, as she quickly pulled the saucepan off the bright orange electric element.

"Alright, alright, take the job," she agreed, partly due to the added annoyance of the potato lava, I'm sure.

Part-time work soon turned to full-time, as my father's positive outgoing personality was quickly valued at the club. After a short while they bestowed the salubrious title of "bar manager" on my father

That was that. Our future for the next fifteen years was sealed in ways we were yet to comprehend.

At first, the new work position seemed like the opportunity my father had been waiting for—until his behaviour mysteriously changed. My father's usual disposition was humorous and loving, so initially when the angry outbursts began it seemed totally out of character for him. My mother was at a complete loss to understand why her husband would leave the house in the morning one person, and seemingly return another. My brother would sometimes quiz my mother, on his arrival home from school, about what may have happened during the day to set our father off—such was the dramatic shift in his personality.

In fact, initially, we partly blamed our mother. Those were early days. None of us were yet aware that our father had fallen victim to the lure of hard alcohol and the long-term pernicious effects it was about to unleash on our family.

One decision forever changed the course of our lives. From butcher to bartender, from sober to drunk, from father to alcoholic.

CHILD SOLDIERS

The back door slammed violently and the whole house shook. I immediately stood motionless and listened for his voice. All my senses were on high alert as I strained to hear the first encounter with my mother, to gauge the level of his drunkenness. I held my breath and prayed for a miracle, but to no avail, as I heard the familiar cursing being spewed at her.

"Please don't swear in front of the children," she pleaded tearfully, as she desperately tried to preserve some semblance of normality for her children.

The request was sufficient catalyst to send him into an abusive tirade about how she was turning the children against him. The sound of a smashed dinner plate against the kitchen wall, summoned us to our defensive positions. We ran from our bedrooms and arrived in the kitchen in record time, just in case he decided to push her around.

My eldest brother took his usual stance in between

them and barked orders at my sister and me, like a general directing his troops. "Out of the way. You will get hurt."

I obediently ran to my safe place, the corner of the sleep-out—the closed-in veranda at the back of our house. I crouched with my knees pulled up under my chin and buried my face. I prayed for the argument to end as salty tears streamed uncontrollably down my cheeks and cascaded over my bony knees. I felt too small to be any real help and as the argument escalated, I prayed more fervently.

"Please God make him stop, please God make him stop."

My prayer seemed to fall empty to the ground as the sound of the argument raged on. I was too young to understand the complexities of free will and faith. I chose to disobey my brother and abandon my hiding place when my mother's voice suddenly changed from a scream to more of a high-pitched shrill. I arrived on the scene in the hallway and found my father had somehow momentarily pushed my brother and older sister aside, and secured a tight grip around my mother's throat with his hands. The image of her terror-filled eyes bulging as she struggled to find breath does not leave a child's memory easily. He always had an almost superhuman strength when he was drunk, which made our task as young children seem almost impossible.

I jumped straight into the melee and now the whole family was a tangled mess of arms and legs as we rolled down the narrow hallway, like a game of family Twister gone horribly wrong. The sound of cracking plaster as our backs fell against the wall mingled with grunts and groans, pierced the still night air. Suddenly, I heard my voice which had somehow risen above the violent, noisy commotion.

"Please stop, Dad! Please stop," I yelled frantically.

For a brief moment, in the midst of those twisted bodies and muffled screams, our eyes met, and the miracle I had prayed for suddenly turned up. My father unexpectedly released his vice-like grip from around my mother's throat. I would like to think that his love for us as a family broke through in that moment, but I will never know.

He yelled his usual threats of intimidation as parting gifts and stomped away in defeat. For now, the danger had passed.

We retreated to our bedrooms like child soldiers, each of us needing our own space to rest and recover. I could hear my mother crying softly through the bedroom wall, exhausted from the physical battle that had just played out in our home. I tiptoed into her room and lay next to her ever so quietly. I twirled her fine soft red hair between my fingers until it felt as smooth as silk—the twirling possibly more for my comfort than hers—and watched her breathing slowly settle as she fell asleep, albeit fitfully. I stayed awake with my tired eyes fixed firmly on the bedroom door for as long as I possibly could, just in case my father returned. I frequently spent nights of my childhood sleeping in my mother's bed, on guard.

I woke to the sound of the alarm clock. It was 8.15 am. Late already. I reached across my mother who was still asleep, slammed the button to stop the annoying buzz and slowly dragged myself out of bed.

My first mission was to locate a clean school uniform from the mountain of discarded washing on that dreadfully messy green lounge on the back veranda. The light green checked fabric of my uniform was not easy to spot amongst the array of coloured clothing in the pile. I finally caught a glimpse of it and plunged down and pulled it free from the bottom, and accidentally knocked some clothes onto the floor in my rush. I had no time to gather them up, so I kicked them roughly out of the way and they lay on the floor as evidence of my rushed morning. My mother usually ironed my uniform, but never on mornings that followed physical battles the night before.

I suddenly felt anxious when I remembered I hadn't done my maths homework. I worried the teacher would stand me at the front of the class as punishment, his condescending voice highlighting my supposed lack of discipline. I hated maths anyway—I couldn't for the life of me fathom numbers. Memorising times tables was of no value to a kid just trying to survive at home. I snatched a banana for breakfast from the kitchen bench and as I munched on it running up the hill to school, I started to devise a plan to miss my maths class. Perhaps I could feign a headache, or I could convince Anne to climb through the broken school paling fence, and hang out at her place. Anne was my best friend and she lived right next door to our primary school.

∽

My friendship with Anne had begun awkwardly when I accidentally bumped into her as we lined up next to each other for a running race at school, one hot, dry Friday afternoon.

"Watch what you're doing!" she grumbled, and glared at me with competitive anger in her deep-green eyes.

"Sorry, I didn't mean to bump you," I said under my breath, too shy to speak up for myself.

She didn't acknowledge my response, so focused was she on her race preparation. I looked down and edged my right foot forward a little over the painted yellow line on the concrete, to gain an advantageous start. I may have been shy and yet I was fiercely competitive.

As we waited for the whistle, beads of salty perspiration rolled down my face and I felt the familiar rush of self-consciousness as it tightened its claustrophobic grip. I despised the hot summer sun because it made my freckles stand out even more distinctly than usual, like someone had taken a brown marker pen and drawn random dots on a stark white piece of paper. I loathed my freckles. It was like they were faults, multiplying beyond my control. A clear complexion somehow weirdly represented a normal, safe life to me.

"Take your mark," the teacher yelled.

I looked down at my pale white legs next to Anne's olive legs, my scuffed black school shoes next to her shiny ones, but mostly, I noticed her confident aura next to my timid uncertainty. And of course, her smooth, unblemished complexion.

"Ready, set," and the shrill of the whistle announced the start of the race.

I was well out front by the first corner, thanks to my sneaky foot advantage. As we approached the old red brick building which housed the principal's office, I had a solid lead. When I finally reached the far end of that dusty playground, I noticed Anne and Peter had caught up to me and we slid around the timber goal posts almost as a threesome. We jostled each other as we ran shoulder to shoulder and pushed ourselves to run faster. I enjoyed the camaraderie of running beside them. I was mostly exhilarated though at leaving the others behind, especially the popular girls.

Peter finally pushed past us with every ounce of boy strength he could muster, to secure a victory. Anne and I followed closely behind in what the teacher described as a "dead heat" for second place.

It was after the race that Anne shared the secret of the broken paling fence between the schoolyard and her home. She asked if I was brave enough to sneak through with her tomorrow at lunchtime.

Of course I was brave enough. I needed a friend like Anne.

BROKEN FENCES

*O*ur lunchtime escapades through that fortuitous broken paling fence would not only become the highlight of my school day but also give me a glimpse into a wider world that awaited. It required great stealth and careful planning as our agile young bodies crawled secretly through that broken fence, and yet I cannot recall ever being caught for our misdemeanour. Our friends often collaborated with highly creative distraction techniques to keep the teachers occupied.

"Miss, I think I'm going to vomit"—accompanied by convincing theatrical dry retching.

"Miss, come quick, there's a brawl in the loos"—followed closely by someone dramatically falling at the teacher's feet, with all manner of fake injuries.

Peter, with his olive skin, light brown wavy hair and green eyes, was the best distracter of all, although perhaps my bias lay in the fact that Peter was my first real boy-crush. I was well aware that all the popular girls liked him and I had very little to offer, apart from my fast running skills—which was hardly an overly feminine trait.

And so it followed that a great number of our friends became experts in distracting the teachers, their willingness motivated by the usual promise from Anne —"You can come to my house on another day"—using her smooth tone of voice in a smart manipulative way.

Of course, the promise was never made good. Consequently, we were always on the lookout for willing new helpers who would believe Anne's promise. It was relatively easy to find gullible kids in our Grade 2 cohort, because Anne was popular. Everyone wanted to be her friend and yet out of the motley crew of country girls she had chosen me, with my skinny legs, red hair and freckly pale skin. It was a mystery to me and yet we bonded in childlike innocence. Two girls from vastly different backgrounds, who didn't mind a few splinters and could both run like the wind. Actually, climbing through the fence always ended with splinters, and yet that was a small price to pay for the cold Lime Coola cordial that greeted us in her warm, expansive family kitchen.

The first time I slipped through that broken fence, I entered a world far removed from my own, a little like Alice in Wonderland discovering the rabbit hole. A double storey, white Cape Cod house with a red-tiled roof sat on an acre of manicured green lawn. The house loomed into view as I stood up from crawling through the fence on that very first day. I could scarcely take it in, for I never dreamed houses like that existed.

Anne ran around the back of her house to find the hidden spare key, and it was then that I saw the full-size tennis court sitting alongside the swimming pool. The pool was that transparent aqua colour that you only see in magazines for posh holiday destinations, and the wooden pool chairs, though weathered, oozed decadence.

I immediately started to panic. *I can't be friends with this girl.* I tried to appear unfazed by the opulence, but I'm sure my worried face may have momentarily betrayed me. Anne interrupted my insecure thoughts by slamming down two red plastic cups filled to the brim with the elusive lime cordial we had risked life and limb for. I was calmed momentarily by the zesty flavour of the lime as it sizzled on my tongue. We smiled at each other, proud of our daring adventure.

Despite my insecurities about our differing social status, my friendship with Anne continued to grow, nurtured by the fact that we both discovered a natural talent for hockey. Initially, we were intrigued by the fact that we needed sticks, shin pads and mouth guards merely to survive the brutality of the game. We were initially pushed into the fierce sport by a domineering sports teacher.

"You can run fast. Here, take this stick, and stand over there with the hockey girls." The teacher pointed in the direction of all the tall girls in my grade who were already standing under the blue gum, chatting confidently, with their hockey sticks draped over their shoulders.

The tall, confident girls seemed to have a shine to them, a translucent sparkle when they giggled. I was relieved to see Anne standing amongst them. Anne wasn't tall like the other girls, but she sported smooth olive skin, bright white teeth and blonde hair. This was enough to qualify her acceptance into the popular group. I was Anne's best friend, which secured partial tolerance for me. Our running talent had not been tested in formal races, but rather through observation of our success in a game called "red rover" which we played during our lunch breaks.

From the very first afternoon of swinging that hockey stick, I could hit the ball with incredible precision. A natural talent seemingly emerged from nowhere. It lifted me above my family problems during my school years and gave me an identity. I was suddenly "the skinny kid who could play hockey" and I was fine with that.

Immediately, the tall sparkly girls were impressed by this skinny, flat-chested redhead who could belt a hockey ball the length of the field.

It soon became evident that only tough girls played hockey. Any trace of my femininity was quickly devoured in the physical encounters which regularly involved a ball to the face or a heavy clash of bodies during a tackle. The irony was that as a child I never felt tough and yet, somehow, here I was—seemingly fearless on a hockey field. A contradiction, really. Perhaps, inside the parameters of that rectangular grassed field inside those white painted side-lines, I was free to disconnect from reality, even if it meant chasing a frightfully hard red leather ball that at times could bruise your shins beyond recognition.

I loved the competitive nature of the game, the elation of overcoming an opponent in a tackle, and delivering the ball safely between the goal posts, announced by a loud, cracking thud as it hit the wooden back board.

The side-line was usually filled with school friends, teachers and my long-suffering supportive mother, who would all erupt in cheers when I scored a goal. I was finally in control of something in my life, albeit only a humble hockey ball.

School in the country was often characterised by physical games in the playground, which meant most of the girls developed a toughness equal to the boys to survive in the rough and tumble of school life. There seemed to be very little supervision from the teachers, who usually stood eating their lunch in the shade of a distant gum tree in an effort to escape the heat.

Anne regularly joined in games with the boys which were characterised by physicality, red rover being one of her favourites. I joined in willingly, as it gave me a chance to stand next to Peter again, although I was under no illusion that he ever really noticed me. As the two teams lined up opposite each other, roughly fifty metres apart, one or two players were selected to be the bulldogs in the middle. The captain of each team would take turns calling out "red rover cross over!" whereby everyone would run for their lives trying to evade the catchers in the middle. There was very little holding back. If caught, you could be fiercely tackled to the ground, where grass and dirt would imprint themselves on your knees and elbows. Speed and agility were your only hope of survival in this game, and fortunately Anne and I had both.

"I'M PICKING MY TEAM FIRST!" Anne yelled as she arrived in the playground still munching on her shiny green apple with her cordial bottle safely tucked under her arm.

Confidence seemed to ooze from the pores of her skin. I immediately looked down to the ground and started drawing circles in the dirt with the tip of my school shoe. I licked my chapped lips and flattened down my curly fringe with the palm of my hand, a ritual I performed when I was nervous. Attractive girls all seemed to have straight smooth hair, not unruly curls like the ones that framed my face. I looked up to see a throng of kids closing in around Anne and could hear a chorus of voices vying for her attention.

"Pick me, Anne! Pick me!"

My hopes disappeared with each fresh voice joining the fray.

Anne stepped back from the group of girls pushing

against her and put both hands up to stop their advance. I stood on the periphery of the group and pulled on the hem of my uniform to try and cover my knees which were covered in warts, intermingled with the new adolescent hairs poking awkwardly out of my skin. I had threatened to shave my legs since the hairs first rudely appeared and yet my mother held the belief that I was far too young to begin such a beauty regime. I tilted my head to the side and tried to appear less desperate, and it was then, above the commotion, that I heard the sweetest sound.

"I'll take… Sue first."

Anne pushed through the crowd and pointed at me. I wasted no time running to stand behind her like a faithful puppy. I felt like my world had suddenly become lighter and our friendship was finally cemented into place, once and for all. She looked over her shoulder at me and flashed her mischievous smile.

"We're going to win," she declared.

But I had already won, well before the game had even started.

I WAS CONVINCED that Anne's popularity was partly achieved by her smooth pigtails, and I was determined to replicate her appearance and tame my curls at any cost. I developed a nightly ritual whereby I would tie a scarf tightly over my sopping wet hair before going to bed, and sleep in it till morning. It was terribly uncomfortable, like sleeping with your head in a vice, really. I would often wake with a headache.

My mother was horrified at the lengths I would take to eradicate my curls, often expressing great concerns for my health.

"You cannot sleep with wet hair Susan. You will get a chill, or worse—pneumonia," she pleaded.

Of course, I ignored her concerns, and was fully convinced that the threat of pneumonia was a small price to pay for the popularity that would accompany my straight hair. The forecast of rain however was always problematic; one short downpour could destroy all my efforts from the night before. Over the years, my hair would continue to be an important and even slightly obsessive part of my self-image. Whilst my physical body was uncooperative and embarrassingly underdeveloped, I could exert some degree of control over my hair, which in some small way perhaps made me feel more powerful. The red colour of my hair was another matter entirely, and that would be addressed later in life with the miraculous assistance of peroxide.

The hairy legs were also tackled around this time in quite the rebellious way, despite my mother's thoughts on waiting till I was in high school.

"Only cheap girls shave their legs!" Mum said.

I had no idea what she meant by cheap girls, but the girls with the smooth legs sure seemed to be having the most fun. I was perhaps one of the last girls to finally shave my legs. It had become a matter of social acceptance, and I needed all the help I could get! One night,

I secretly locked the bathroom door, and determinedly removed those curly protruding hairs once and for all. I emerged from that bathroom with smooth legs, lavished in copious amounts of baby oil, and walked to my bedroom with an air of defiance.

Supposedly, I was one of the cheap girls now, and I couldn't be happier.

A FAIR PORTION of my upper primary school years were spent playing at Anne's house, especially during the school holidays. Their home sat on a half-acre block and it seemed so vast compared to my small backyard.

It wasn't that I didn't have other friends in my primary school years. In fact, others were equally as important.

Perhaps Anne's friendship is immortalised in my memory with greater prominence as it represented everything I longed for in my own childhood.

We spent our days running freely, climbing gum trees and diving into their pool to cool off on hot days. In fact, Anne and her twin brother would play with such wildness and freedom I would at times feel overwhelmed by their utter abandonment to the world around them. Abandonment is meant to characterise childhood and yet it was a strange, unreachable concept for me. At times, I would feel myself slipping into the delirious freedom of play until, quite unexpectedly, I would be interrupted by an irrational sense of impending doom. It was like someone would sneak up from behind and tap me on the shoulder to get my attention, just to remind me that I had more serious things to dwell upon.

Somehow, I thought that if I abandoned myself fully to the world around me, everything I was supposedly holding up would come crashing down. The need to hold back disaster has remained a constant companion since my childhood and has turned up at the most unexpected times, like after the birth of my second child, when it appeared masquerading as postnatal depression. But I have jumped too far forward. My battle with postnatal depression can wait for now.

My childhood taught me to hold the reigns of life tightly and always have a backup plan. Anne frequently let go of the reigns and she had little need for a backup plan.

As a young child, I was intrigued by Anne's father, who was a well-known doctor in town. He would arrive home late in the afternoon wearing a brown tweed checked jacket, shirt and tie and carrying a well-worn tan leather case. I would often ponder what was inside that life-giving leather case.

The contrast between him and my own father was so extraordinary that at times I would find myself staring at him from a distance. He was a quiet, reserved man and yet warm in his interactions, always saying hello and enquiring about our day. I was incredibly shy and found it hard to make eye contact with him. But that was not unusual for me. I also held quiet fears that he may find out about my father's drinking and stop Anne and me playing together.

Shame spoke to me often, always with the same repertoire of accusations. The loudest and most insistent, however, was always the thought that I was not good enough to be best friends with a doctor's daughter.

FOR BETTER OR FOR WORSE

*T*onight was well beyond our capabilities as child soldiers.

The sound of a smashed dinner plate found us all colliding in the kitchen at once—an army summoned to action. The sky-blue-painted kitchen provided a contrasting background for the bright mix of colour dribbling down its walls—yellow corn, green peas and brown mince. The cheerfulness of the colour palette seemed such a contrast to the violent way in which the food ended up there.

"You call this shit 'food'?" he shouted.

My determined spirit rose up and I wanted to yell and tell him to make his own damn food, but this would have endangered us all, so, as always, I adopted our family mantra: "peace at all costs".

Dad followed up with his teacup, and as it smashed and joined the pile of plate fragments already on the floor, we knew. Mum looked across the kitchen at us and we were familiar with her unspoken message. It was going to be one of those nights.

We hastily grabbed a jumper from our bedrooms and assembled at the back door like a swat team about to embark on a secret mission.

"To the car now. Hurry hurry!" Mum whispered. We frantically ran down the back concrete stairs to the garage where our old white Holden lived.

Opening the wooden doors of the garage was a challenge most often conquered by my older brother, as the timber had swollen from the weather and was wedged tightly in its frame. A fairly decent heave with a simultaneous kick at the base of the door would usually see it spring open. The swift timing of the manoeuvre was critical when your raging father was standing at the back door, hurling threats.

"Lock your doors," Mum screamed, as she crunched the gears and navigated an unusually quick reverse up our steep concrete driveway.

I pressed the door lock and the sound of the click gave me an immediate sense of comfort and safety.

I would discover in later years that the abject fear that takes hold of you as a child when you have to run for safety in the middle of the night, does not relinquish its power over you easily.

Darkness would become my enemy. I would be forced to confront and overcome an irrational fear of the dark that had developed as a young girl.

As we reached the top of the driveway, my father, who had doubled back through the house and was now on the front patio, continued yelling abuse in a last desperate attempt to stop us. As we drove away, I watched in horror as he reached the footpath and stood unashamedly raising his fists and yelling abuse. I looked to see if our neighbours' lights would come on because of the loud commotion, and yet darkness continued to shroud their homes.

This was the generation where people minded their own business and a misguided sense of privacy prevailed.

It was always such a massive relief to drive away and feel safe in the cocoon of our family car. I was crying and my brother and sister snapped at me.

"Be quiet, Susan, and let Mum drive." They spoke almost in unison, with a finger raised to their lips.

I felt the familiar thud of the railway tracks under the wheels of the car, which signalled we were heading to the other side of town, towards my grandmothers' house. We passed the bakery where they made the best cream buns, and I was briefly distracted by the thought of those tantalising buns with their sugary cream and strawberry jam oozing out the edges. We turned the final corner into Macleay Street and parked out the front of my grandmother's house.

"Wait in the car. I won't be long."

My mother opened the red steel gate slowly to reduce the squeaking sound it made, and walked tentatively toward the front door. As well as watching her steps in the dark, she was trying desperately not to disturb the neighbours.

Neighbours in the 1960s seemed to be of a different breed. Whilst they were close and supportive, they also at times held fierce, unspoken judgements about each other. Well this was the way it was in my grandmothers' street anyway. Everyone seemed to know your business. Appearances were everything. I recall my grandmother secretly hid the fact that she had a part-time cleaning job in town. She had devised an elaborate plan whereby she left the house dressed up in her finer clothes, carrying a bag with her cleaning clothes hidden inside. We all loved and admired our hardworking grandmother.

I rubbed a small patch of fog off the window with my hand so I could see more clearly as my mother gently knocked. The door opened but only partially, and we could hear soft weeping. I expected my mother to be immediately embraced in a motherly hug and ushered inside. I had already chosen in my mind the spare bed I was going to safely slide into.

But this was not a scene from some sentimental movie where the main character is rescued. My grandmother brought a finger to her pursed lips.

"Be quiet, the neighbours will hear you," Mardie whispered with an uncharacteristic angry tone to her voice.

Alarmed that my safe, warm bed was not going to eventuate, I rolled down the car window so I could hear more clearly.

In disbelief, I heard the final part of the hushed conversation unfold.

"Go home to your husband," she said sternly, and waved her arm in a dismissive motion.

The opened car window formed a kind of frame

around my mother, and it captured a silhouette of her grief-stricken shape in the darkness.

I saw her place her face in her hands as the realisation dawned that her own mother was not going to provide the safe haven we so desperately needed tonight.

The most unnerving aspect of revisiting this memory has been trying to reconcile the cold actions of a grandmother who was always warm and loving to me as a child. How could she send her daughter away when she needed her most? I was angry at her lack of bravery. Why couldn't she summon up the courage to go against the social tide? My anger quickly diminished when I realised it was shame that stopped my grandmother from saving us that night. The same shame that haunted my mother was also attached to her. She had fought hard to build the family that had been taken from her as a child, and my mother's predicament threatened to destroy all that she had built. The thought of being thrown back into the grief and rejection of her childhood perhaps overrode her emotions as a mother. A silent melody from her past was no doubt also playing in the background of her life.

The drive to my uncle's house was deathly silent apart from intermittent sobs from my mother. I hated it when she drove the car crying, because her emotions would cause her to weave erratically on the road. Fear had gripped me again, partly due to her driving and partly because I thought she may give up the search for a safe place and take us home.

"Please don't go home. Let's sleep in the car, it's not that cold." I used all my persuasive powers birthed from a childhood of fear.

"Just be quiet, and let Mum concentrate!" snapped my brother and sister in unison.

~

I HATED BEING THE YOUNGEST.

No one sees you.

Unless of course you make a fuss or resort to being the family clown. I had developed well-honed skills in both roles but, tonight, making a fuss was definitely my best option to keep us safe, and I was determined to cry up a storm.

We were not going home.

"Please, Susan, stop crying!" My sister resorted to a gentler approach to calm me.

In hindsight, I understand why they needed me to stop crying as it only further distressed my mother.

The little girl was merely trying to keep us safe.

~

MY SISTER WAS the middle child. Four years older than me, she always seemed so much more grown up than I was. Her personality was so different to mine. Conscientious at school and helpful to the teachers, always well-behaved. I was so envious of her early adolescent growth and full, round breasts. The white sanitary pads she carried around in her school port only added to her grown-up status, although initially I was never really sure what she actually used them for. The pads had recently been handed to her secretly, amidst hushed tones and a sympathetic look from my mother, whose cryptic explanation had left me none the wiser.

"Your sister is a young woman now," Mum whispered in the hallway as she slipped into my sister's bedroom with a white chemist bag and closed the door behind her.

Well, quite frankly, I couldn't care less if she was a young woman now. I was furious about the fact that it was a stinking hot day and my cousin and I had been left abandoned and waiting on the hot front pavement of our home. My sister had promised earlier to take us to the Olympic pool to cool off and now our plans were falling apart at the seams. An impromptu visit from my aunty, who also tiptoed secretively into my sister's bedroom with a knowing smile, only added to our confusion. The pool adventure was suddenly called off, with no consultation or explanation, and I silently vowed I would never need those horrid mysterious pads myself.

I conscientiously added them to my prayer list.

As we continued the drive from my grandmother's

house, I watched the trees rush by in the darkness. My vivid imagination created evil images in the shape of the branches and it only served to fuel my already irrational fear of the dark.

"I'm tired and cold," I said as I flopped dramatically across the back seat of the car.

I imagined being in a normal family, one that didn't have to drive about in the middle of the night looking for a safe place to sleep. I thought about Anne in her smart white house, tucked warmly into bed.

My tears however, proved successful, and before long we pulled into my uncle's driveway. He greeted us at his front door, his face holding a look of both empathy and pity, mixed together, and ushered us in out of the cold. The warmth of his house immediately hit my cheeks.

Just seeing my uncle with his kind, strong presence was enough to steady our wavering world.

He would become the father we never had.

Uncle Rex had been abandoned by his own family when he chose to marry an Anglican. His love for my mother's sister, sealed his supposedly-sinful fate.

As a young butcher needing board he had stayed at my grandmother's home, and it was during this time that he and Greta met and fell in love. Dating back in the 1940s was a different experience. A chaperone was required to accompany dating couples, something we humorously refer to as "third wheeling" nowadays.

Greta's twin sister, therefore, was forced to act as chaperone, tagging along with them to many social gatherings such as church dances on a Friday night and the movies.

The role of chaperone was at times a lucrative arrangement for her twin. Some Friday nights after the dance had ended, Greta would bribe her sister with sixpence to run home so she and Rex could wander hand in hand, unaccompanied. Her sister would hide behind the kurrajong trees that lined the street their home was in, no doubt with her reward of sixpence clutched securely in her hand, waiting till the lovebirds came into view. My grandmother would of course have been horrified had she known of the business arrangement between the sisters.

It was not long before Rex asked for Greta's hand in marriage, which should have been one of the happiest days of their lives.

Their joy was quickly extinguished by the religious hypocrisy of the day. They later told the story of his Catholic parents when they arrived at the front of my grandmother's home, to try to deter him from the wrong path he had chosen. They stood on the footpath and wouldn't cross the boundary fence for fear of being spiritually tarnished, calling out to their son to change his mind about the young heathen girl he was about to marry.

It must have been a heart-wrenching scene, and yet Rex stood defiantly by his fiancée and watched his own flesh and blood walk away, disowning him. They lost a son that day, but my family gained a saviour.

God's plans were far greater than man's religious divide, and I learned a valuable truth from that story.

The goodness of God and His plans stand resilient and unchanging, regardless of the frailties of man.

School days were always hard after nights gallivanting around in the car. I arrived slightly late as usual and tried to look like I was recovering from a headache, by dramatically holding my forehead as I strolled toward the school grounds. Anne was standing there, waiting dutifully at the school gate, looking fresh faced with her forever-beaming smile.

"Hockey practice this afternoon!" she shared excitedly, and we ran together to our classroom to avoid being too late.

Walking through the school gate with Anne was like entering a different world where I was free to be just me, with no one to save but myself. We ran up the concrete stairs two at a time, laughing as we slid the last five metres in our school shoes, always racing. We knocked tentatively on the classroom door, standing with our shoulders physically touching for extra courage, and waited for the teacher to stop speaking.

Miss Frost was my favourite teacher with her long black silky hair, short checked woollen skirt and gentle smile. I could always keep up in English, regardless of missed homework, as fortunately I had an uncanny knack for spelling.

"Where have you been, girls?" she enquired firmly,

yet with a warmth to her tone that always made me feel safe.

Anne always had a convincing reply, so I looked to her.

"Sorry, Miss, but I left my hockey stick on the oval and we had to race back and collect it."

We stood with our hands behind our backs to show respect and add further credibility to our story.

"Take a seat quickly please, girls, and take out your book. It's silent reading."

Miss Frost spoke with slight agitation, as if she knew the truth but had cleverly chosen avoidance over conflict.

Silent reading was always a lifeline. It gave me the gift of time and space which I so desperately needed to switch my brain from worry and fear to the freedom found in the routine of the school day and in the stories themselves. A time to imagine, a time to calm myself and escape into a different place. I was inexplicably drawn to fairy tales, possibly because of the ever-predictable happy endings. At the time, I would not have realised why these storylines appealed to my young self and yet it's painfully obvious now. I was desperate for my own happy ending.

I always found it hard to disengage from my book at the end of silent reading in class, because somehow the story in the book was a place where all my fears didn't exist. Closing the pages of that book seemed to reopen the floodgate and my brain would fill again with torrents of real-world thoughts. The real world, where our family was trapped and no one was coming to save us.

The end of the school day came surprisingly quickly, although the thought of hockey practice didn't greatly enthuse me, because I had to get changed into my sports clothes. By upper middle primary years, the change room had become my greatest social nightmare. It seemed grossly unfair that most girls had budding breasts standing proudly under their soft cotton sports t-shirts, whilst I was still dealing with a chest that resembled two flat pancakes. To add further insult to my dilemma I had to get changed in full view of their snickering glances. Therefore, my flat chest and I always chose the furthest corner of the room where the walls provided some degree of privacy. I had been asking my mother for weeks to buy me a trainer bra so at least I could pretend there was something lurking under there, even if my plan was to shove crumpled tissues into the bra.

Anne had started to develop too, which made my self-confidence plummet even more. She insisted on getting changed right next to me, as best friends do. I looked discreetly across at her one afternoon to check out the progress of her breast growth as she unashamedly threw off her uniform with not a care in the world. It was then that I saw it. A light pink, lace-edged, trainer bra sitting neatly on her golden skin. Damn it, I thought.

Of course, Anne's mother was organised.

The other downside of hockey training apart from my poor body image issues was the fact that it made my school day longer and this delayed me getting home to my mother. My father's roster at the club was always at the forefront of my mind. A particular shift that rostered him on at the club between 7 am and 2 pm had always terrified me, because it gave him an opportunity to hurt my mother while I was still at school. As a child, the worry of my mother's safety was like holding a heavy weight up above my head, somewhat like a weightlifter. A weighted bar that could descend upon me at any time, when my arms tired of holding it up. Most of the time I had learned to hide that burden of worry, and yet at times a teacher, or in this case a discerning hockey coach, would notice my disposition change.

"You feeling okay today, Suzy?" she said as she walked beside me.

"Yeah, I'm good thanks." I would run swiftly back to the centre line to start the next training exercise, without making eye contact.

I did not have to wait long before my fears were realised and that weighted bar came crashing down, one bitterly cold afternoon. I raced to the school gate to get ahead of Anne so she couldn't see our old car—a common ritual if my mother was picking me up from school. My mother always parked dutifully around the corner, a fair distance from the school gate, abiding by my childish request. In hindsight, I suppose her acceptance without protest of my somewhat self-centred instructions on where to park was a reflection of the sense of shame, we both carried. We were both hiding.

My brown school port was always heavy and

awkward, but more so on the days I was juggling my hockey stick. In my haste, my legs got tangled up in my hockey stick and I fell heavily to the ground. I looked down and noticed my knees were grazed and bleeding, but I didn't want to keep Mum waiting so I quickly wiped them with my hanky and hurried on.

As I crossed the road toward the car, I could see a bright multicoloured silk scarf draped loosely around her neck, and she was wearing unusually large dark sunglasses that I was unfamiliar with.

My heart lurched.

I ran to the car and hurled my brown port and hockey stick into the back seat of our car. I climbed in the front next to her, and we sat, holding hands, both unable to speak.

She wept, while my silent anger rose.

After some time, my mother found her words.

"I'm sorry Susan," she whispered in between tears.

I didn't know what she was apologising for.

"It's okay, Mum."

But it was far from okay. I pulled my uniform discreetly over my bloodied knees. My injury suddenly paled into insignificance compared with the bruises on my sweet, defenceless mother. Initially, I was too scared to look directly at the dark red-purple marks that peeped out from the edges of her silk scarf, so I glanced sideways to try and lessen the reality of her injuries. If I don't look, I thought to myself, perhaps I could stay safe just for a moment longer, in the innocence of childhood denial.

My denial was short-lived when I arrived home to a

sea of broken glass all over the front patio, and the damning evidence that my father had literally pushed my mother out the front bedroom window.

Remnants of her makeup powder lay scattered on the mustard carpet and on the wooden dresser, where she must have been standing before he unleashed his anger. My mother was protective of her makeup, treating it like gold, such was the price—and here it lay, scattered amongst chunks of glass.

Later that night, after the shards of glass were picked up and my mother was finally resting, I stood quietly at my father's bedroom door and stared at him as he slept in a drunken slumber.

I wondered what pain drove a man to such addiction and violence.

But mostly, I thought about how we would be safe if he was dead.

THE FAMILY ANTHEM

My uncle's lounge room was overflowing with family. Extra chairs had been awkwardly shoved into every available inch of space so we could all sit together. Togetherness was compulsory at family gatherings, with no exceptions—and my father hated it.

I watched him sit on the outside of the misshapen family circle that weaved erratically around the edge of the room. He deliberately turned his chair slightly outward in an act of defiance, almost as if he was ready to make a quick getaway. His legs were crossed and his arms folded, high up on his chest, protecting himself. Guilt had attached itself to him and regardless of the love surrounding him in that erratically woven family circle, he assumed the position of an outsider. He crossed and uncrossed his legs, seemingly forever agitated.

This was a social setting where hard liquor was never available. While beer and Great Western Spumante may have flowed at our family gatherings, there were never spirits—the culprit for my father's demise. There was an unspoken rule in place, I guess.

One of my uncles was a gifted musician and he called loudly from the piano where he was seated, across the room to my father, trying to rise above the cacophony of voices and laughter.

"You ready mate?"

Immediately, Dad's deep brown eyes filled with tears. His body turned slightly to face the family circle he was so desperately rejecting, and a forced smile broke out across his face. I looked at him with confusion because he had such a depth of compassion and love inside, though it lay deeply buried. Music had a way of disarming him.

"Sing up," everyone encouraged.

Dad stood to his feet and walked towards the piano where he rested his elbow on the top and began to sing his favourite song.

Nat King Cole would have loved our family get-togethers. His songs were the heartbeat of our gatherings.

My father's favourite was *A Little Street Where Old Friends Meet*, a song which speaks of being accepted amongst old friends and family regardless of your circumstances or social standing. A song of sentimentality that broke down my father's walls and gave me a glimpse into his true self.

It seems a strange mix that someone so violent when drunk could also be so vulnerable and warm. Perhaps this paradox was a key to understanding the pain of addiction my father endured. I have come to realise that addiction is separate to the real authenticity of a person.

I kind of sensed, even as a young child, that he desperately wanted to be the father we needed, but he just couldn't seem to get himself there. Looking back, the secrecy and lack of support that surrounded his addiction disturbs me greatly. He must have felt like he was continually drowning and no one was throwing him a life raft.

As damaged as my father was, and regardless of the pain he caused, he was accepted by my mother's extended family—which was testament to the unconditional love and forgiveness that could always be found there.

Sadly, he didn't know how to fully accept that love.

My father's voice cracked with emotion as he sang. I do not presume to know the complexity of his emotions, although I suspect his grief ran deep at the loss of love his addiction was stealing from him. Whether he deserved the acceptance from my mother's extended family was another matter entirely, and yet, as he sang his favourite song, he was accompanied with vocal gusto by the only people that probably ever really cared about him.

And if there was one thing you could count on from my big, loud, sometimes inebriated extended family, it was that they would always treat everyone the same. My father included. Music masked our pain and brought us together as we crowded around that old piano and sang the same songs that over the years would become more like family anthems.

I liked standing close to my uncle to watch his fingers float effortlessly across the keys. He was a builder by day and a gifted musician by night, who could play by ear without the need for a single lesson. My uncle quietly loved the attention. He demanded silence in the room before he would begin. He would place his hands on the keys, which was a signal for the chattering to cease as he waited for our undivided attention. I adored the songs he sang, even though they were not of a modern genre, for they spoke of a romantic love I had never seen between my parents.

Music always seemed to bring my mother so much joy. She must have secretly envied her sisters' marriages and yet she lived each day determinedly pouring out every ounce of the love that was meant for her husband into her children.

We received a double portion.

Her love saved us.

The final song of the day was always the same, a *piece de resistance* of sorts. It was for Rex and Greta, the Catholic and the Anglican whose love had flourished over the years, despite religious prejudice and family abandonment. Fittingly, the song was titled *Because*, the lyrics describing a love shared between two people who believed in a higher power who had brought them together for a lifetime. A song that would eventually bear witness to a long and happy sixty-five years of marriage. A marriage that shone brightly.

> "Because, you come to me
> with naught save love,
> and hold my hand and lift mine eyes above,
> a wider world of hope and joy I see,
> because you come to me!"

As a young, shy, fearful girl, I sat amongst the loud singing and found a place of peace and safety.

The words resonated within me and every year we sang them together it helped a young girl believe in "a wider world of hope and joy", too.

SEASIDE SOJOURNS

Our extended family drove long distances from Dubbo to holiday at seaside places like The Entrance or Toukley where we would dip our country toes in the salt water, ride waves with our foam boogie boards and suffer shocking sunburn after misjudging the severity of the summer sun reflecting off the white sand. Our country swimming escapades in a wide, fast moving brown river were no preparation for the crashing intensity of waves in an ocean. Neither did our previous log rides in the fast current of the river rival the challenges of the unpredictability of the waves.

And yet, we loved the sea. The smell of seaweed, the way the salt caked on your skin and the traipsing through the hot sand at the end of the day.

I liked the idea of driving long distances. It felt like we could drive away from real life.

Perhaps the real excitement of a holiday lies in the anticipation of creating something new. Family holidays offered a much-needed change of scene for us. The most difficult part of going on holidays with a father you couldn't depend upon, though, was actually getting to the destination. My mother would often drive long portions of the trip as Dad slept in the back seat and my brother sat up front offering his adolescent support.

The most harrowing part of our journey was the section of narrow road over the Great Dividing Range that stood between Dubbo and the sea. A notorious stretch of the mountain known as Bells Line of Road was named after the young 19-year-old explorer, Archibald Bell Junior, who first navigated it—and yet, as children, we naively thought it was named after the sweet-sounding bellbirds that lived there. At the first chime of their distinctive call, we would all furiously wind our windows down to feel a little closer to the elusive creatures. They seemed to call to us as we wound our way through their home and safely down to the base of the mountain.

One night as we approached the infamous stretch of road that always loved to deliver thick fog, a massive storm hit with such incredible force that the heavy rain made visibility almost impossible.

"I can't see. Should I pull over?" my mother asked.

Her request for help was met with silence from the back seat. I tried to shake my father awake but soon decided he was better off asleep anyway. Less trouble. I thought it strange how my mother still expected her husband to help after years of him not being available for her. Was it a desire to catch a familiar glimpse of the man she married? A longing for him to stand up again? I suspect so.

"You're going well, Mum. Keep driving," my brother said.

We continued to crawl slowly along the plateau section of the pass following Uncle Rex's tail-lights, all silently anticipating the descent—a serious challenge for our old Holden at the best of times. Without warning, the windscreen-wipers screeched to a halt and stopped working.

"I can't see a thing," my mother screamed.

"Pull over, Mum, as soon as it's safe," said my brother, taking charge.

Uncle Rex returned to check on us, after he noticed that we had stopped on the side of the road. He opened the boot and found an old towel which he wrapped around my brother's arm. He explained to my brother that he had no choice but to lean out the window and manually move the wipers back and forth with his arm until we reached the bottom of the hill. The remainder of the pass was therefore conquered with my brother leaning precariously out the window, battling cold sleet and fog whilst my mother navigated by following the constant red tail-lights of our ever-dependable uncle.

My father slept, entirely oblivious to the whole windscreen-wiper debacle.

My husband will attest to the fact that I can at times be the passenger from hell. My desire to control any vehicle I am riding in is perhaps another leftover childhood trait. I am unable to unhitch myself from the burden of keeping everyone safe.

This role of the rescuer remained with me for some time, until I recognised what it was. My life at times resembled that of someone who has lost their bearings running from one spot fire to another, extinguishing flames, in an effort to avert a full-blown blaze.

At times, my sons have been the beneficiaries of my prompt firefighting skills. My initial reaction was to rush in and rescue them at the first sight of any sparks that might fly in their lives. Over the years, I have worked hard to overcome this hypervigilance, because the trouble with rushing to smother the embers of other people's fires is that it delays them learning to extinguish those flames themselves.

BEACH HOLIDAYS WERE such a contrast to our country life that our inexperience in the surf was often rewarded with a fierce dumping onto the hard sand on the ocean floor. I was petrified of the waves and preferred to stay close to the shore. Uncle Rex, however, was not fond of allowing fears to hold us back. He would insist on taking us beyond the break line.

"It's calm once you get out past the waves, Suzy. Come on."

He grabbed my hand firmly, letting me know there was no tolerance for my youngest-child antics. I'm not entirely sure what qualified Uncle Rex, a butcher from the country, to be a reliable expert regarding the ocean, but we had developed an unquestioning trust in him.

"I'm scared. The waves are too big."

I dropped my lower lip in an effort to persuade him. This behaviour never worked around him, and there was rarely any mollycoddling. Perhaps deep down he knew we needed to be tough to survive.

"You will be fine, Suzy. Come on now." This time he left no room for argument.

We walked, initially, until the water was about up to our hips. When it became too deep to stand, the dreaded "under and over rule" would begin, always the most daunting part.

"Now, when I say over, you jump with me and if I say under, we will dive under the wave."

My eyes locked on the incoming waves and I gripped his hand like a vice, trying to predict their height. As each wave approached, they looked like huge dark green mountains rolling toward us. I trusted him to call over or under, and somehow spluttered, jumped and dived my way beyond the breaking waves. My bravery was always rewarded by a peaceful, rolling ocean, and we would lie on our backs and float freely over huge hills of aqua water, anchored safely by the grip of my uncle's hand.

We all discover sooner or later that life brings waves. Sometimes, we have the benefit of seeing them rolling toward us and have time to draw in a deep breath and prepare. At other times, they crash upon us with no warning at all and suddenly there we are, floundering in the impact zone, breathless.

You would think a tough childhood would have made me more resilient, and yet this was not my experience. My inability to deal with emotional upheaval has at times paralysed me. I felt like I had been left completely drained of any strength. How ironic that this young child who fought so hard to protect her mother had been left feeling almost stripped bare of courage.

This contradiction left me as an adult with no option but to rebuild from the ground up, to find a foundation of unwavering truth that I could trust.

My faith in God was stirring again.

Easter was my favourite time of year. The autumn morning sun drenched my grandmother's back garden. The May bushes, flush with sweet, fragrant white flowers, seemed to fill the air with hope. It was the perfect setting for an Easter egg hunt with my cousins, a family tradition that my grandmother had nurtured over many years.

We would all assemble near the old red brick garage for the obligatory family photo first. The excitement amongst us was palpable. Being one of the youngest meant I had to battle hard to outwit my older cousins and locate those hidden chocolate eggs. I needn't have worried, as there was always a plentiful bounty. A trail of white fluffy cotton wool pieces strategically scattered on the grass and amongst the bushes offered clear clues as to where the Easter bunny had supposedly hopped.

The feeling of absolute joy at the first glimpse of those brightly coloured, foil-wrapped eggs hidden amongst the garden is one of my most treasured childhood memories.

I believed in that fluffy white rabbit far beyond the normal childhood age. I suspect it was because those Easter mornings in my grandmother's garden were about far more than finding chocolate eggs.

LIFE AND LOSS

He was never sober when we needed him. The night my beautiful silky terrier died in his woollen basket on the back veranda was no different.

I hadn't seen death before.

I kept softly shaking him to make sure he wasn't just sleeping. I sat next to his basket in shock, crying, and tried to understand for the first time the finality of a life passing. I was around twelve years old.

My mother gently covered his head with the blanket from his bed, which signalled to me that he really was dead. She quietly murmured something about how he was at peace now. She hugged me and stroked my hair and as I leaned into her for comfort, we were abruptly interrupted by my father. He reached down from behind us and snatched Sammy roughly from his basket, blanket and all.

"Get the shovel, I'll bury him!" he snapped at my mother, as he walked down the stairs to the backyard, with my most precious companion tucked under his arm like an old rag doll.

It was late, dark and bitterly cold.

"Wait till morning," my mother pleaded, seeing the absolute distress on my face.

I watched through the louvres at the back of our house and could see the silhouette of my drunken father in the darkness as he started to dig a hole with an old shovel in the back corner of our yard, right next to the patch of sweet corn I had planted. I recall being strangely distracted by the thought of my dead dog's remains perhaps leaching into the roots of the corn, and I silently vowed never to eat it again.

The dread that he was going to put my still-warm, silky haired dog in a cold, deep hole was almost unbearable. I started running towards him as car lights flooded the backyard. Uncle Rex had arrived with my cousin to help, no doubt in response to a secret distressed phone call from my mother earlier.

I screamed at Dad to stop digging and my mother managed to snatch Sammy's body back. She cradled him in her arms as if he was still alive. My cousin, my Uncle's only daughter, quickly assessed the scene. She ripped the shovel from my father and pushed him clear across the lawn.

On reflection, this was very brave for a twelve-year-old, although she was always a strong, courageous girl.

Her superhuman strength that night was forged from strong family connections where, over the years, our cousins had become more like sisters and brothers.

I watched as she continued to dig the hole that

would hold my faithful dog. My father retreated, accepting defeat in the face of extended family numbers.

We stood in the darkness together and my mother knelt down and gently lowered Sammy into that awfully dark pit. Uncle Rex covered him over with fresh dirt.

I cried differently that night. It was real and deep, and my cousin kept her arm around my shoulders until I stopped.

Mum assured me that we would make a cross in the morning and put some flowers on Sammy's grave. My father had successfully welcomed me to the cycle of life and death through a lens of dysfunction and insensitivity.

I RECALL the day my father brought our purebred silky terrier home for the first time.

"Susan, come here," he called urgently from the backyard.

I raced through the house and down the concrete stairs to see my father swaying with a tiny puppy in his arms.

"He's yours." He smiled proudly at me.

I was so happy because my father had bought me a gift and yet my mother was infuriated by the impulsive drunken purchase. (I would later learn I had actually inherited the dog by default when my father's mother rejected the gift.) I appeased my mother by promising to take full responsibility for the dog and begged her to let him stay.

By this time, the silky-haired little puppy had nestled into my body and I was smiling broadly, using my most persuasive youngest-child head tilt.

"Oh, alright Susan, he can stay." She relented, probably realising the joy it would bring into my world.

"I'm calling him Sammy," I said.

Dad winked at me with an intoxicated gaze. It proved to be one of the few loving connections we shared during my childhood. Sammy became a constant and faithful companion in my uncertain world. Perhaps, deep down, my father had known he would be unable to defeat his demons, and the puppy was his way of giving love to me, the only way he could.

I would sneak Sammy into my bedroom and let him sleep on my bed most nights. He had this habit of curling up next to me behind my legs and resting his head on top of my bent knees. I would reach down and stroke his fur for comfort on those nights when my father paced wildly about the house, as I waited for him to finally relinquish his rage and fall asleep.

I CAN'T REMEMBER the actual day Anne left. There were no long drawn-out goodbyes, just awkward adolescent hugs between two twelve-year-old girls.

We barely spoke of her impending move to a boarding school in Sydney until it was almost upon us. I suspect the childhood guilt Anne felt for leaving her friend was too complicated to process, and her mother probably told her not to say too much. We laughed and played our way through the summer school holidays and I was blissfully unaware of the separation that was to come.

Then, towards the end of our long hot summer spent climbing trees, riding bikes and swimming in her posh aqua pool, Anne took my hand and we ran up the stairs to her bedroom. On the bed was a tan-coloured leather suitcase with her clothes packed neatly inside. I could see a pair of new black leather school shoes on top.

"I'm leaving tomorrow, starting at a new school in Sydney. But I'll be back on the holidays and I promise we'll play."

Tears welled in my eyes, but I didn't want Anne to see, so I looked away. Neither of us could cope with the emotion of the moment, so we ran back down the stairs and resorted to the familiarity of our hockey sticks, belting balls relentlessly at each other.

My mother cried when I told her Anne was leaving, feeling my heartbreak like it was her own, as mothers do. "I'm so sorry, Susan. I wish I could afford to send you to school in Sydney too," she whispered across the kitchen table.

I didn't understand why my mother was lamenting, such was my naïve view of the world. I wasn't even sure where Rose Bay was, and I could barely pronounce the name of Anne's new school, Kambala, anyway.

The whole thing made no sense to me. Why did Anne need to go to a school in Sydney when we had everything we needed right here? Hockey fields, drive-in movie theatres, fifty metre swimming baths, and family fine dining at the Hing Wah Chinese restaurant.

"Where will Anne live in Sydney, Mum?" I asked.

"She will live at the school, darling, in a boarding house." She wiped her eyes with a Kleenex tissue, trying to regather herself.

Always trying to regather herself. I reached across the table and held her hand and tried to reassure her.

"It's okay Mum, please don't cry. I don't want to live in Sydney and sleep in some smelly boarding house."

And I meant it—I wanted to stay at home. I was just twelve years old and didn't want to leave my mother. I looked into her weary eyes and I could see the burden of our battle starting to take a greater hold on her. I looked more deeply at her face and noticed new lines around her eyes that were not there before. Her shoulders seemed to rest lower than they had previously.

I would probably never leave home, I quietly thought to myself.

My childish-self felt betrayed that I had to leave primary school and navigate the unknown landscape of high school without Anne. I recall an overwhelming sadness persisted for quite some time.

I would walk past her house on the way to my new high school and sometimes her mother would be tending to the garden with her large-brimmed straw hat on. She would wave enthusiastically and then drop her head to avoid full eye contact. It was clear from her demeanour that the bond between us was fading. I suspect she felt sad that I was left behind and had decided it best to cut ties quickly, for fear of extending my heartache.

Anne was true to her word and the first few school holidays she came home and we played, just as she promised. As the years progressed though, she came back home less and less, opting to visit her new boarding school friends over the holidays.

There was no doubt that Rose Bay was changing her. My best friend from primary school was slowly disappearing and a sophisticated young woman was emerging. Anne dressed in expensive clothes and spoke with an articulate accent that made her sound like she was a different person. I knew I was falling behind. As each year passed, we saw less of each other, until finally our bond was broken completely and we lost contact.

Shame settled upon me again. Perhaps I wasn't good enough for Anne after all.

Many years later, when my mother was diagnosed with cancer, a grown Anne would walk back into our lives again, as an up-and-coming oncologist from Sydney. Anne treated my mother with the same warmth and kindness that resided in that seven-year-old girl I had climbed through a broken school fence with more than twenty-five years earlier.

Rose Bay had indeed been the making of her.

I REMEMBER the afternoon we got the call that my grandfather had passed away at eighty-three years of age and my grandmother, summoned us all to her house. We gathered in her front room and waited. She strode into the room with a determined gait that showed she had dealt with grief before. This was a woman who had been orphaned as a young girl and had lived through two world wars, so there was no succumbing to tears, just an explanation that our grandfather had passed away after sipping on his cup of tea and eating his afternoon sandwich.

"I would like each one of you to go into his bedroom and say goodbye on your own," she instructed.

I was barely fifteen years old and the thought of seeing a dead body horrified me.

"I never want you to be afraid of death," she quipped at us as she left the room.

I was petrified of death and that's all there was to it. I was determined I was not going in to see my grandfather lying dead in that bed. I imagined the scene and the very real possibility that half a ham sandwich might still be protruding from his mouth, mid-bite.

As each family member came out of the room with a distressed gaze upon their face, I became even less convinced to enter his room and bid farewell. I was fairly confident I would get out of the request—being the youngest and all—and consequently I was the last one, standing in the corner hiding behind my mother, when my grandmother's eyes settled upon me.

"In you go Susan, hurry along dear," she said as she

pointed in the direction of my grandfather's room. "The funeral directors will be arriving soon, there is not much time left."

Funeral directors will be arriving soon. What do funeral directors even look like, I thought to myself. I walked slowly toward the door and froze as I saw him from a distance lying propped up in his bed. My mother took my hand and walked beside me, thankfully breaking the "go in alone" rule that my grandmother had so strongly declared earlier.

I stood near the bed and his face was ashen and I remember thinking there was not one drop of life left in him. I glanced at his bedside table where the half-eaten sandwich remained on a small plate with light pink flowers on the edge, and some tea, possibly still warm, sat in the bottom of a cup.

I thought how strange it was that you could be here one moment and gone the next, right in the middle of chomping on your ham sandwich. I leaned in tentatively and kissed his cheek, not because I wanted to, but because I felt it was expected. His skin felt cold and clammy on my lips and I immediately regretted my decision to extend such a generous farewell gesture.

I walked out of that room and was haunted by the image of his forlorn frozen face for years.

And yet in spite of the deathly image imprinted in my memory, I had been gifted with precious insight.

My grandfather's physical body seemed totally void of life and this only served to add to my belief that when we leave this earth, we must enter another place.

We all stood in the front room as the funeral directors, dressed in dark suits with their heads bowed respectfully, carried my grandfather out the front door.

Only then did my grandmother cry.

TEENAGE BLISS

I only wanted one present for my thirteenth birthday. For him to be sober.

I stared in the mirror at the blue-flowered dress with its high frilled collar that my mother had sewn on her old foot pedal Singer sewing machine. My mother would often sit for many hours making our clothes, and the sewing machine could be heard humming away at various bursts of speed. At times, she seemed to lose herself in the mindfulness of the task and the comforting hum of that old Singer, as if escaping the world she found herself in. She was indeed a very talented dressmaker and had made the dress especially for my thirteenth birthday dinner.

As I stared in the mirror looking at the detail in the dress, I felt ugly. It wasn't the dress itself making me feel that way, but rather my under-developed body and freckled skin. No one had ever told me I was pretty. Well, my mother had said it numerous times, but that didn't really count to a teenage girl. I was waiting for my father to say it. He never did.

I had always wished I had my sister's olive skin and full breasts. I was so envious of the fact that she could wear one of those bikinis with rope ties at the sides, sunbaking at the river on her bright yellow white-frilled beach towel, and not look like a boy.

Here I was, entering my teenage years with nothing to show for it.

A transition to teenager, and yet I sure as hell wasn't transitioning.

I was like a butterfly trapped inside its chrysalis.

All my friends whispered secretly about boys and periods, while I sat timidly listening, smiling and trying to pretend I understood what they were talking about.

I didn't really want to grow up anyway.

Mum still needed me.

I had grown to hate birthdays. In fact, celebrations of any kind made me nervous, as they just provided another excuse for my father to justify his drinking.

He was meeting us at the restaurant after work, which in itself was a recipe for disaster. I was lovingly seated in the middle of the table at the restaurant, surrounded by aunts, uncles and cousins, while the seat at the end of the table was left empty—for my father. My brother was not there as he had already escaped to live in Sydney.

I missed him.

I opened my gifts, trying to appear interested, but I was distracted, waiting for his arrival. I hid my anxiety with a fake smile I had learned to perfect over the years, to mask my pain and try not to add to my mother's.

I needed her to stay strong.

My mother and I frequently exchanged glances across the table, knowing what each other was thinking and yet outwardly hoping for the best.

Always hoping.

We heard his loud arrival as he walked up the stairs to the restaurant, and before we saw him I knew he was drunk. All my dreams for a normal teenage future seemed to vaporise in that one brief moment as he leaned over to kiss me for my thirteenth birthday.

"G'day darlin'."

My cheek felt the sting of his rough bristles and the aroma of whiskey was heavy on his breath.

"Don't I get to sit near my daughter for her birthday?" he aggressively announced.

"Kevin, please," said Mum.

My mother jumped up in her usual peacekeeping fashion and directed him to the chair at the end of the table. The whole extended family peering at him perhaps made him rethink his anger for now, and I could sense my mother's frustration and the utter grief she felt for her daughter. My mother seemed to grimace her way through these childhood milestones, determined to create some semblance of normality for her children.

Uncle Rex stood up from the table abruptly to make the obligatory family speech and created a timely distraction.

"If everyone could raise their glasses, I would like to

propose a toast to Suzy on her thirteenth birthday," he said loudly, regardless of the fact we were in a restaurant with other people dining.

We tentatively raised our glasses, as we knew from past family celebrations the actual culmination of the toast would be a long way off. Uncle Rex had always placed great importance on speeches and consequently they were long drawn-out affairs. Perhaps the importance was not so much the speech itself, but his desire to fill the role of father in our lives.

"As your godparents, we just want to say how proud we are of you darling, and you look beautiful tonight. It's nice to see you all dressed up in a frock, rather than your hockey gear." Everyone laughed.

My father returned to the table from the bar, another drink in hand, just in time for the end of the speech, and while everyone else clapped, I noticed an angry glare he tossed toward my uncle. I felt a sudden sadness for my father, whose anger was simply an outworking of the shame he must have felt about being unable to turn up sober to his daughter's birthday.

Sadness that he couldn't be the man he wanted to be.

He smiled at me from the end of the table with pride beaming from his glazed, dull eyes and I caught a glimpse of his love for me, beneath the addiction.

I sent an awkward smile back feeling emotionally confused by this new-found empathy for my father.

An empathy that had gate-crashed my thirteenth birthday.

It was strange, but I always liked the start of a new day. I guess it was another chance that things could change. A childlike resilience.

"His mercies are new every morning," my mother would declare, so I figured if her godly wisdom was ever going to prevail, it was definitely going to happen in the morning and I sure wasn't going to miss it.

I enjoyed breakfast too, especially if it had been a peaceful night before, as my mother would be up and about, fighting back against the chaos and determined to be the mother she longed to be.

I loved sitting at the brown vinyl-topped table, even though it was too big for our cramped kitchen and had to reside pushed hard up against the wall. It was on sale just before Christmas hence the cheap price, which far outweighed the fact that it dwarfed the space it was in. We all thought the high-backed bright orange vinyl chairs were fancy, though they did little to disguise the fact that the table was oversized, with their splayed steel legs that always tangled whenever they were pushed in or out. My father's drunken anger was often further provoked by those cumbersome chair legs, and consequently the table edge recorded every angry shove with numerous dints. I would sometimes run my finger along those dints while eating eggs on toast for breakfast and reflect on the night before. Not surprisingly, I would lose my appetite. I was a poor eater.

"Eat up, darling, you're late for school and the

protein's good for you," Mum would encourage, with her soothing tone.

Breakfast with my mother in that cramped kitchen before school became my peaceful interlude. The poached eggs and freshly squeezed orange juice represented far more than physical sustenance for me, they fed my emotional self which was far more depleted than my skinny frame.

I could always trust breakfast, but not dinner, for by evening, the kitchen changed personality dramatically if my father had been drinking. Many a dinner plate met its demise smashed against the wall, if my father deemed the food to be of a poor standard or not to his liking. The image of my mother crying, kneeling down to sweep up chunks of broken dinner plates with a dustpan was heart breaking.

More significant was the message it was sending me about being a woman in the world, and I quietly seethed at the unfairness of her life.

I WOULD SOMETIMES HEAR my mother selflessly shuffling around in the semi-darkness of early morning, getting dressed to go to her cleaning job at a local motel. The Merino Motel was a brick, U-shaped building with a grassed interior courtyard where guests would sometimes gather to sit in the sun.

My mother made strong friendships with the other women who were also working tirelessly at that old motel, probably all needing extra income to support their families. During school holidays I would sometimes accompany her and see first-hand the way those women worked and laughed alongside each other. They were like a sisterhood, sharing the joys and sorrows of their lives as they stripped dirty sheets off beds and remade them with crisp white linen ones. Whispers, tears and unbridled laughter would echo through the courtyard as those women worked their way through each room restoring it to order and encouraging each other to continue on.

When I heard my mother preparing to leave for the motel, I felt such empathy for her, particularly in the winter when the mornings were deathly cold. I would pull the blanket up over my head to warm my face, as my cheeks felt chilled compared to the rest of my warm body. After drifting back to sleep for a few hours, I would usually be abruptly woken by the sound of the old Hoover vacuum cleaner being hauled roughly around my bedroom floor by my brother. As the eldest, he was responsible for us while my mother worked on the weekends.

I loved safe Saturday mornings. Dad was at work and we were home alone, free from the imminent threat of violence and happy to just be kids.

Perhaps the most vivid memory from this time was the chocolate cake my brother would make for us. In the beginning, his first attempts resulted in a cake that resembled a hard piece of black rock, although we never told him. And yet, he managed to perfect the recipe over many Saturday mornings and eventually created the most mouth-watering chocolate cake a young girl could wish for. There was something so comforting and predictable about the aroma of that cake being baked every Saturday morning. We sat together eating huge pieces, laughing together, and with each delicious bite the cares of the world drifted away, just for a time.

Then the chores were completed—mostly by my brother and sister, as I would deliberately take my time eating my cake to avoid helping, as the youngest often does. The real excitement would begin after the chores were done and the cake had been devoured. Our favourite game could only be described as a cross between wrestling and martial arts, utilising an old straw broom from the laundry cupboard as our preferred weapon of choice.

The lounge room was cleared of furniture to create the perfect wrestling arena. The old brown vinyl recliner remained in the corner of the room and was transformed into a judge's chair by piling countless pillows from every bedroom in the house. As the youngest, I was regularly placed on this mountain of pillows to conduct the judging, deemed far too young to wrestle by my brother and sister. In hindsight, I suspect this chair was merely an elaborate plan to distract me, and their real motive was to keep me out of the game.

"Let me wrestle, it's not fair!" I would scream from the top of that mountain of pillows.

"You're too little, Susan, you will get hurt."

"Please, please, please let me wrestle," I screamed with tears in my eyes now.

I watched as they continued their game, laughing and rolling around the mustard coloured carpet, trying to secure each other in a headlock. I became more furious with each wrestling manoeuvre I had to watch—and it was then I hatched a plan that would finally get their attention.

Never underestimate the youngest child.

I silently slipped off that phony judge's chair and straight out the front door, completely unnoticed. I knew exactly where I was heading and that was straight to the motel where my mother worked to report to her directly about my unfair treatment. I ran for the first two blocks to get a head start on them, in case they noticed I was missing.

The most challenging part of the walk for an eight-year-old girl was always going to be slipping past old Mrs Stedman's house, which sat on the third corner block. There's always that one old dilapidated house that stirs the fertile imagination of young children—Mrs Stedman's house was that house. She believed in a whole array of superstitions, one of which was that wearing the colour green brought bad luck upon you. I stopped running just before her fence to catch my breath, and it was then that I glanced down at my attire and noticed the dreaded bottle green jumper I was wearing. As I approached her house, I could see from a distance she was sitting on her front veranda, in a cane chair, with a red-checked woollen blanket over her knee. Her long grey hair was swept up in a loose bun with wisps that fell wildly about her shoulders. I hoped she was dozing in the winter sun and I could sneak right past, until a high-pitched voice shattered my wishful thinking.

"What are you doing near my house?" she shrieked,

throwing the blanket from her knees. "You're wearing green! Get away, get away from here." She launched herself out of her chair and headed toward her red steel front gate with surprising briskness for her age.

My fast walk quickly turned into a desperate run and my heart beat wildly inside my chest. I was so afraid, I crossed the road without properly looking for cars and heard the sound of a car horn as I reached the other side. My fear produced another surge of anger at my brother and sister for not letting me play their stupid wrestling game. It's their fault I had to run away and was almost cursed by a witch, I thought to myself.

The youngest rarely takes responsibility.

The remainder of the walk took another half hour before I finally reached my mother's workplace. This of course gave me ample time to rehearse my dramatic arrival. I was determined my brother and sister were going to pay dearly. As I walked sheepishly along the side path to the hotel, I found Mum cooking breakfast for the motel guests in the kitchen. She looked up from a smoking fry pan full of bacon and eggs and immediately turned off the hotplate to sweep me up into her arms.

"Oh sweetheart, what are you doing here?"

I watched her face whiten when she realised I had come alone.

This was 1969. The year an eight-year-old girl called Vicki Barton had vanished in broad daylight in Lawson, New South Wales, and struck fear into the heart of every parent. I was the same age as Vicki and I distinctly remember the day she disappeared. Our country town was soon emblazoned with posters of this sweet young girl dressed in her lemon cardigan, police desperately searching for clues to her whereabouts. Being the same age at the time, I remember being deeply troubled by her disappearance for some time.

A few minutes later my brother and sister came running frantically into the motel grounds and came face-to-face with our mother. She wasted no time launching her attack.

"I cannot believe you two would lose your little sister and not realise she was missing. Do you know what could have happened to her?"

They both went to speak, but were overridden.

"She could have been run over by a car or anything!" she yelled angrily.

I smiled over her shoulder at them and poked my tongue out feeling wonderfully vindicated.

"Well you can walk your sister back home and buy her an ice block on the way."

"Alright, we will. We're so sorry Mum."

They glared at me and took my hand squeezing it hard as silent punishment. We walked home awkwardly, mostly in silence as I licked my red icy pole.

The next Saturday, I wrestled.

CHANGING OF THE GUARD

"You will not leave this house!" screamed my father.

He had spent most of the afternoon drinking in his recliner chair in the front lounge room.

I leapt up the back stairs two at a time. I had been in the backyard, busy belting hockey balls against the back concrete wall when I heard the raised voices. I arrived in the front room to see my father standing toe to toe with my brother, who was now seventeen years of age and had developed a far greater physical strength than previous encounters. I felt incredibly proud of him in the midst of such a verbal assault, that he was able to keep his aggression in check. I also knew his restraint was being sorely tested with each new insult.

"Who do you think you are?" yelled my father, as he leaned in closer to my brother's face for added dominance.

My brother leaned closer to my father as a show of strength.

I stood in the doorway, instinctively knowing the argument was going to escalate. Ironically, throughout our childhood, we had never been physically hurt by our father as he had always released his anger solely upon my poor defenceless mother. Maybe we suffered the odd bump and bruise as we stood between our mother and father in physical battles, but we were never specifically targeted by him.

His weapon of choice against us as children was typically verbal. Accusations that we would never amount to anything or that we never finished things we started. Accusations no doubt birthed from his own weaknesses.

I was shocked to watch as the argument suddenly turned physical between them. So desperate was our father in his bid to stop my brother leaving home, that for the first time ever, he reached across and grabbed him by the throat, pushing him back against the wall.

"Let him go, Dad!" I screamed frantically.

As my father's hands tightened around my brother's throat, my gentle-natured brother was forced to stand up to him and use his new-found physicality.

With one almighty shove, he hurled our father across the length of the lounge room. He fell backwards into the double glass doors, causing them to spring open onto our front veranda. Fortunately, my father regathered his footing.

I suspect that almighty shove from my brother had been building for some years as he had been forced to witness the cowardly violence that had been unleashed upon our mother.

This final encounter not only finished the argument that afternoon, but it also stole perhaps the last remnants of their relationship.

My father stomped away, a defeated man in more ways than one. Physically and emotionally he had lost.

Addiction had stolen any chance of a normal relationship with his eldest son. The realisation in that moment that it was now too late must have been crushing not only for my father, but my brother also.

When my brother left for university in Sydney, I know he didn't want to leave us behind, for he would have felt like he was deserting his post, and yet we never felt that way. It was time for him to leave and my mother would not have had it any other way.

It was just a changing of the guard. As the younger ones, we remained.

We remained, like soldiers in the trenches, protecting our mother.

My mother cried for months and months after my brother left home. The sadness of the separation was no doubt intensified because her son had filled the role of a male she could depend upon in her life.

My older sister stepped into the protective role seamlessly, and I continued to pray for our miracle.

The fact that my brother was free to pursue a career and go to university was a miracle in itself, not just because of his chaotic childhood but also since he had narrowly escaped compulsory conscription to the

Vietnam War in 1971. The stress of the ballot was no doubt worse for mothers who understood the reality of war, having lived through one themselves as children.

My brother and his friends naively thought being conscripted might be a post-school adventure, a gap year of sorts, before they entered the real world. Little did they know; a different reality awaited the young men randomly selected by what would later be referred to as the "death lottery".

The number of twenty-year-old men eligible for call-up exceeded the number needed for military service, so a ballot was organised. Marbles numbered with birthdates were placed in a barrel. The twice-yearly ritual played out in our dining room. The transistor radio was finely tuned to the ABC, and placed firmly in the centre of our dining table.

Our dining room was every bit as cramped as the adjoining kitchen and yet in spite of its size, it was deemed the fanciest room in our old house. This was due to the glass-topped dining table with light-coloured wood legs and a matching sideboard table, with black and lemon glass doors. My mother was proud of the furniture, which she paid off on a long-term payment plan. Anyone we needed to impress was always guided into the dining room. I was always so grateful for the saving grace of that room and its respectable furniture as it offered some semblance of pride, nestled amongst the backdrop of poverty that so blatantly shone from the rest of our home.

The broadcast was 10 am. My mother sat with her elbows resting on the table, leaning on her forehead, eyes closed, in a prayer position. She repeatedly leant across the table and obsessively checked the volume dial to ensure it was on the highest setting, for fear of missing the birthdate numbers. My brother sat beside her, with a somewhat young-nonchalant attitude.

One particular December morning, when my brother was just shy of twenty, the ballot narrowly missed his birthdate by one day. My mother cried tears of joy when my brother was spared from the horrors of war, and yet she also wept for those young boys chosen at random whose lives would never be the same.

Domestic opposition to the war itself was building, however, and a group of brave women had begun supporting an anti-conscription organisation aptly called Save Our Sons.

My mother made a personal vow that December day to vote for any political party that would abolish conscription, regardless of her political persuasion. The following year in December 1972 the newly-elected Labor government ended conscription as one of its first acts. Our sons were safe once again, including my brother.

I MISSED my brother terribly too, especially the sound of his band jamming in our old weatherboard garage. I had spent many nights hiding near the garage amongst the white-flowered May bush, peeping through a small hole in the fibro wall to listen to repeated renditions of *The Letter*, by The Box Tops. I knew the words by heart, as the song was a feature in their very limited repertoire.

The muffled, over-amplified lyrics would ring out into the night, powered by an old second-hand speaker that crackled because the volume was no doubt well beyond its capabilities.

I would sing along unnoticed, and stare at the lead singer who was so handsome with his long dark hair. The band seemed a world away from my existence and gave me a sweet reprieve in an otherwise fearful childhood. A glimpse into a world beyond mine, a glimpse of what might be waiting on the other side of the chaos.

My brother was the drummer and he conscientiously held the beat, a constant in the band just as he was a constant in our family—the steady one. Of course, they could only practise in our shed on the nights Dad worked late, for fear of exposing our family secret. My brother would call time well before our father was due home, so the band were packed up and gone before his arrival, in case he was drunk.

He was mostly drunk, and yet every night I continued to hope that he would arrive home sober. I continued to pray. Every now and then, reality would give way to my prayers.

I HEARD the door to the toilet on the back veranda slam in urgency and then the heaving began. I looked at the clock: it was 2 am. A smile broke out across my face as I lay in my bed. I remember feeling so happy the old fella was sick. Peace at last.

I threw off the bed covers, raced to the toilet and pressed my ear against the door to hear more clearly. To my delight, a deep retching sound met my ears, and it was the sound of a miracle—the sound of a peaceful sleep, the sound of safety. I tiptoed into my mother's bedroom to bring her the news.

"Dad's spewing his guts up," I whispered, and crawled under the covers next to her.

We smiled at each other unashamedly in the darkness. Relief rolled deliriously over my body and I drifted off to sleep like a normal kid.

From time to time, following long binge-drinking sessions of around three months, my father would fall violently ill and be bedridden for a number of weeks. He would literally vomit for days and days as his liver struggled to cope with the constant assault of alcohol on his body. He would be unable to eat anything.

I remember looking at his weak, fragile frame as he wandered aimlessly around our home. It was such a sharp contrast to the strong, violent, rampaging man that usually dominated our lives. As a family, this was our reprieve. A time of desperately needed peace, to rebuild our courage and reconnect with life more fully. If we had an important exam or sporting event, we would secretly hope it would fall during the time our father was sick because that gave us the best chance of succeeding.

As a young child, I felt happiest when my father was most sick.

What a collision of confusing feelings to understand.

More shame crept in.

The most utterly disheartening part of this cycle, of course, was the hope that would rise each time my father was ill. There were many cycles over a period of fifteen years where hope would rise and fall, and our father would remain trapped in the addictive prison of alcohol. It was torturous to watch and even more torturous to endure. I suspect the most harmful consequence of this loss of hope as a child was a despondency that I carried into my adult years.

A fearful view of the world was silently building, undermining my courage and stealing my hope.

I started to believe that perhaps mountains were unconquerable after all, and valleys impassable. Childhood beliefs that took hold as I watched, helplessly, as my father failed time and time again to overcome his addiction.

I walked into my adult years with the belief that no one could overcome their weaknesses.

DERAILED

My need to rescue people was subtle at first. I found the perfect subject to repair and restore when I met my first boyfriend at university. He had experienced a somewhat-similarly-difficult childhood from the absence of his natural father. He was tall, dark-haired and had a ruthless sense of humour. His ability to make me laugh attracted me to him instantly and we would spend the best part of the next five years laughing our way through university and beyond. But laughing with someone is rarely enough. At some point, the laughing stops.

This was my first real boyfriend and I had no clue about healthy relationships. Looking back, I was a naïve girl from the country with a complicated mix of values and insecurities, and a damaged view of men. Not the greatest framework on which to build my first romantic relationship. My brokenness was initially masked by the typical university behaviour of excess drinking that tends to accompany this transition from adolescence to early twenties.

It was not till much later that I started to realise I had possibly been attracted to a man who was broken, purely because of my need to fix him.

Well not him specifically, but my father.

Of course, in the beginning, I never understood I had a need to repair those around me.

Needless to say, as we unknowingly tried to mend each other, our relationship fell victim to the lack of self-worth bequeathed to me by my father and by the absence of his. The break-up sent me into a spiral that would take some time to recover from. The aftermath broke open a whole vault of beliefs about men that I had developed as a young girl. Beliefs that were hijacking my choices and emotions.

False beliefs, that had been lying dormant.

Beliefs that I didn't even know existed.

The cracks from my childhood were opening up like hairline fractures beneath the surface of my life.

THE NIGHT I met my future husband felt like someone literally reached down and pulled me out of a deep pit of miry clay. I was twenty-seven years old and I knew from the moment we met that he was different. We literally bumped into each other in a crowded bar in the city, as I was chatting with my work colleagues.

"I'm sorry," he said, as he smiled warmly and his blue eyes glistened.

For some reason, I was intrigued by his straight white teeth and was quietly impressed by them. Perhaps I inwardly contrasted them with the misshapen yellow teeth my father had.

"Hello there." He leaned closer to me to speak above the noise of the crowded space we found ourselves in.

A sudden, inexplicable ease rested upon me that I had never felt before, and we talked for hours. By the end of the night, an unusual bond had formed between us. Our lives took different paths for the next few months, until—quite literally—we bumped into each other again. A couple of dinner dates followed and we were soon inseparable. Best friends.

Just how I managed to recognise the qualities of a man who could be trusted and didn't require a rescue and repair job was indeed miraculous in itself, and yet I knew instinctively that this man was my future.

I remain eternally grateful.

There was a greater power at work, gently weaving its way amongst the ashes of my childhood.

A power I was yet to fully understand.

I WAS adamant I wasn't doing a bridal waltz. I relented due to the persuasive powers my ninety-year-old grandmother wielded due to the respect she had gained over the years.

"It's tradition," she said, smiling at me with sentimental tears in her weary eyes.

I agreed to dance.

The lights dimmed—apart from an overly-bright, intrusive spotlight in the centre of the dance floor.

I immediately regretted my decision.

The room fell silent and the chatter of wedding guests gave way to the screech of chairs being turned to gain a better view of the bride and groom. I stood slowly and yet I still managed to awkwardly get caught up in my veil, which almost ripped my headpiece off.

Every fibre of my being wanted to run.

I had always thought the bridal waltz was overrated anyway. Does a couple's chance of marital bliss depend upon their ability to struggle through an embarrassingly awkward display of dance steps, while everyone looks on, silently pretending not to judge their lack of finesse? My husband sensed my anxiety and he took my hand firmly and led me to the centre of the room.

We stood in the spotlight, waiting for the music to begin. As we stood, I lifted my head to look into his face and suddenly, I was transported back to that young girl again, peering into the face of an angry father, twirling waltz steps on my tiptoes on the back veranda of our home.

The child inside me lurched.

I immediately dropped my head, gratefully distracted by the gentle movement of my white organza dress with its full skirt swinging freely. The sound of the music and clapping brought me back to the present moment.

I found the courage to look up again and, this time, the warm face of my husband beamed back at me.

The child inside me settled, for now.

The contrast of my childhood dance with my wedding dance was so vastly different that it was almost too overwhelming to process. As we waltzed, tentative hope rose within me, for the first time in my life, and the realisation that perhaps a new dance had begun.

My tale is not new. Many of us are dancing to steps learned from a sad childhood. Holding fast to a rhythm of unworthiness, fear and shame.

A new dance had to be choreographed if I was to find hope and freedom for a better future.

I was now a wife and soon to be a mother.

These new roles would bring inevitable changes. Changes that would gradually begin to expose the cracks from my childhood. Cracks I didn't even know were there.

I had successfully bandaged my childhood scars in outward achievements. Gaining an education, followed by successful teaching positions and the ability to make friends with ease. Eventually, however, adhesive bandages start to peel back at the edges after they have been on the skin too long. Beneath lies a wound that needs air and light to heal. It was only a matter of time before my bandages would fall off completely and reveal the real extent of the wounds beneath.

Having babies can do both strange and wonderful things to a woman's body.

I thought I was entering motherhood fairly well-prepared in comparison to my own mother, who was of a generation that rarely spoke about sex and babies. In fact, I recall sitting with my mother reading my high school biology textbook and she was fascinated by a scientific diagram of the female anatomy. How incredible that even after giving birth to three children of her own, my homework provided the first factual exposure to fully understanding her own body. In later years, she confided in me that she and her sisters had mistakenly thought babies came out of your navel, until a doctor had enlightened my mother as a married woman at the age of twenty. In contrast, I had devoured numerous books about birth and babies.

Most mothers soon discover that all the books in the world can never really prepare you for having a baby.

Nothing except actually bringing that human being into the world yourself.

I was also naïve about how these biological changes can sometimes bring emotional challenges set in motion by childbirth.

It was early one morning after the birth of our second son, following a night of interrupted sleep, when the slow unravelling began. I shadowed my husband, walking very closely behind him as he was about to leave for work. I was carrying our eight-week-old son in a sling, close to my body.

We were living in North Queensland at the time, isolated from family support. I traipsed behind my husband to the car, which was parked in our driveway, contemplating whether to tell him. I felt like I was that scared young girl again, crouched in the corner of our back veranda in our old weatherboard house, desperately waiting for the danger to pass.

But the danger wasn't passing.

"Don't leave me here," I said, as tears rolled down my cheeks.

My husband hardly responded to my plea, putting his briefcase in the back seat of our car. He tossed me a perplexed, disbelieving look.

"I mean it, please don't go to work just yet," I said.

It wasn't that he was lacking empathy, it was more that my sudden overwhelming anxiety was not something he was familiar with.

Quite frankly, neither was I.

Everything slowed down, like my brain was scrambling to catch up with the world around me. I rushed back into the house to quickly place our baby in his bouncer, to keep him safe in case I fainted.

My husband followed.

"I'm so scared," I whispered.

"What are you scared of?" he said, with a flippancy on the edge of his voice.

I could sense an impatience in him. He hated being late for work, and I had always coped.

"Everything," I said.

My rational self was screaming at me to pull it together, but my emotional self was clearly winning the battle.

"But there's nothing to be afraid of." my husband reasoned with me.

These were words from someone who had never fallen into the deep abyss that is called anxiety.

He couldn't possibly reach me.

For he didn't know the way to the place where I was.

I had no idea what was happening to me since I was feeling anxious and not depressed, and so I never entertained the thought of postnatal depression.

My male doctor had certainly missed diagnosing me accurately when I had turned up at his surgery the week before, worried about everything from World War III to the common cold and cancer. You would have thought the strongest clue might have been the two-month-old baby I was holding in my arms, as I sat there incessantly talking about all the things in the world that I was suddenly afraid of. The doctor's oversight would cost me the next six months of my life as I battled to find myself again. I was a far cry from the twenty-something girl my husband had met and married who was independent, capable and headstrong.

Of course, I understand that post-natal depression was not a direct consequence of trauma in my childhood. It was, however, the catalyst for ripping those bandages clean off and reactivating my childhood story.

A story that had left me ill-prepared for both the

challenges of life generally and, more importantly, as a mother.

It was becoming more apparent that the constant childhood companions of fear and anxiety were not about to let go of me without a damn good fight.

My childhood melody had indeed turned up the volume and I was beginning to hear the softest of notes.

As a young girl, I used to wake in the middle of the night with blinding headaches, and for some reason they always seemed to turn up on a Friday night. Perhaps the weekends intensified my anxiety, as my father often worked late on those evenings. I can still remember the awful chalky taste of the dissolved aspirin my mother would bring to my bedside to relieve my pain. She would sit calmly on the edge of my bed and stroke my forehead, reassuring me that the headache would pass once the medicine had taken effect. Even in the midst of the chaos, with my father so often stomping around the house, hurling abuse as the alcohol pulsed through his body, she loved me. Calm tenderness amidst a backdrop of violence.

There was something so frightening about succumbing to sickness when I was a child.

It had very little to do with the illness itself, and everything to do with the fact that I felt weakened and defenceless in a world that needed me to be strong.

Postnatal depression left me defenceless.

In hindsight, my spectacular and unexpected fall had been building for some time and yet I was oblivious to the early warning signs. I had breezed through my first son's pregnancy, birth and early years. My ignorance had in fact fuelled a slightly judgemental view of anxiety. I secretly harboured thoughts that those suffering the condition should be able to just "pull themselves together".

Until I couldn't.

Postnatal depression was like falling headfirst into a black pit with no warning that you were standing near the edge.

And yet the signs were there.

The first was a damaged nerve in my groin from the caesarean operation to deliver my son. The surgical clamps had inadvertently caused a tear in the nerve, and I left the hospital in a wheelchair, with mumblings from the doctors that they were not sure how long it would take to heal, if ever. Just the sort of thing a new mum wants to hear, really.

Fear and uncertainty were languishing in the wings of my life, like an actor waiting patiently to take his place on the stage. The nerve damage meant that at any time and with absolutely no warning, the nerve would catch and send excruciating pain down my leg. This pain was so debilitating it would cause me to stumble and fall. I was so afraid of dropping my new baby I was confined to my bedroom, shuffling around the edges of our double bed, to protect him. The nerve gradually healed after about a month and I was so grateful I could move about the house more confidently.

But all was not well with our young son.

I REMEMBER the first time he coughed in the middle of the night.

It was a cough like no other.

He was sleeping in his bassinet next to our bed and my husband's feet hit the floor before mine. He lifted him up and held him over his shoulder, as the sound of mucous crackled in his lungs. Our son was only four weeks old. We looked at each other with the sort of exchange that waits for the other one to make sense of things. I reacted first of course, such was my heightened response to danger.

"Get the thermometer and we will take his temperature," I said sharply.

Fear gripped me.

We placed the thermometer under his arm and waited. At least we felt like we were doing something. It seemed like we knew so little, and this child's life was in our hands.

HINDSIGHT IS A CURSE FOR MOTHERS.

Even as I write this, I am aware of a certain grief that has found its way to me since my boys have grown up and ventured off into the world.

It is a grief that extends beyond letting go, and far deeper than the feelings of being an empty-nester.

It seems every frailty I see in them, is a reflection of myself.

I have a deep yearning to go back and do it all again, only this time, paying more attention to preparing them for what's to come. How I wish I could return and make them stronger and hold back the pain that will inevitably come. It has taken some years for me to understand that personal resilience is something they must build for themselves.

There are no short cuts or easy routes.

Tough terrain teaches us how to climb.

Tough terrain has delivered unexpected blows to both my sons, in spite of my strongest desires to protect them. I have been forced to stand aside while grief has fallen upon them. My eldest in high school faced the loss of a friend in his year group, and my youngest, just following high school also faced the loss of a young friend.

I was crushed to learn the hardest lesson of parenthood: a mother's love cannot touch grief such as this.

But of course, I was the master of holding back disaster, the young girl charged with the task of keeping her mother safe.

If I could just stay one step ahead, I could thwart danger.

I patted him on the back and he coughed again, only this time I could hear him gasping for air.

My husband rushed to the bathroom and I followed closely behind. We both sat together on the hard tiles in that hot steamy bathroom, taking turns holding our four-week-old son. He coughed and spluttered his way into the early hours of the morning and finally fell asleep in our arms as the sun was rising.

No doctor could diagnose the cough, which continued relentlessly for months and months. His weight was also falling, but at first, I refused to stop breastfeeding. That would have been a failure as a mother. We alternated between doctors, getting opinion after opinion, desperate for an answer. Strangers would hear his cough when I was out and about walking him in his pram, and give us a wide berth for fear of catching some dreaded disease. I would notice the concerned look hidden in their eyes and this did little to allay my fear. I would scurry home with my son, feeling hopelessly inadequate.

Finally, a specialist ordered a test for cystic fibrosis. The test involved taping gauze on a small patch of skin on his leg, to trigger sweating. The sweat is then measured for higher than normal levels of salt. I recall vividly the day we strolled about in the park with our young son in our arms. It was excessively hot and humid.

The closeness of the heat in north Queensland was

suffocating, unlike the dry heat I was accustomed to where a light breeze would float across the western plains and bring relief most afternoons. We had been instructed to walk for half an hour and it seemed like an eternity. We initially made mindless conversation to pass the time as we walked together.

We both quietly prayed for healing for our son.

Faith had found me again, in the darkness.

In fact, faith had found us both again, shortly after we were married. God was building a firm, unwavering foundation beneath us, in spite of our fears.

"What time did we leave the surgery?" my husband's voice abruptly interrupted my thoughts.

I looked at my watch and was shocked to see it had only been ten minutes since we had started ambling aimlessly through the park.

"Let's sit on that bench." He pointed to a wooden bench under a broad weeping fig tree.

We sat and gazed into the distance. We didn't feel the need to speak anymore—conversation would have annoyed us both. I stared at the red brick hospital building and thought about the others who had also anxiously waited for medical results, perhaps sitting on this same park bench. It felt like time had stopped and yet I was aware of people moving about around us.

I was bewildered by the fact that life could "turn on a dime" as my father used to say. And yet, this time I had a man beside me who was predictable and safe. I felt the warmth of his shoulder resting against mine as we sat, and I leaned into his arm trying to absorb strength from him. It's not until you are next to someone with real courage that you suddenly realise the scarcity of your own.

The test for cystic fibrosis was negative.

The test would be repeated twice more by various specialists throughout my son's early childhood as the relentless cough persisted. He may not have tested positive for CF, but he displayed all the symptoms of the disease. Our life soon revolved around the amount of mucous my son's lungs were producing at any one time. Most nights he would sleep in our bed, where we could easily lay him over the edge and thump on his back, using a physio technique we had learned to help him clear his lungs. As he grew older, we made him play sport and relentlessly swim laps to force those lungs to develop normally. I vividly recall watching him struggle to breathe in the pool or on the soccer field, where he would regularly stop to unashamedly cough out mucous and continue on. He was so very thin and pale, we often agonised over whether we were pushing him too hard.

One day, when he was in Grade 3, he strolled to the car after school, slowly with his head down. The sort of head down only a mother understands, where your heart starts to lurch even before you know the full story. He climbed in the back seat and we began the journey towards home with me trying to hold back from asking the inevitable question. I lasted two blocks.

"You seem sad. What happened?" I gently asked.

Tears flowed first, before the words.

"I was sitting in class and the teacher wouldn't let me leave the classroom to cough out my mucous. So… you know how I sound when I breathe, all rattly?"

"Yes darling," I said.

"Well the girl sitting in front of me turned around and said I sounded like a lion growling, in front of the whole class. Everyone laughed." More tears.

"I hate my cough!" he screamed.

For those mothers out there, you would know the irrational feelings that rise up when one of your own has been hurt. I wanted to punch that girl.

The same powerlessness that had accompanied me as a young child had returned to me, only this time as a mother.

The beginning of the journey however is never how the story ends.

We prayed, and the natural world eventually gave way to the spiritual world.

And that ten-year-old son who sounded like a growling lion for most of his childhood is now roaring through life.

He has a perfectly healthy set of lungs and is in fact a brilliant singer.

I DON'T KNOW why my mother didn't leave.

This question lingers more than any other: why she stayed in such a violent, fearful situation and continually risked herself and her children.

I never once saw her pack a suitcase or speak of leaving.

I am certain she felt powerless. Even as a child, I

cannot recall ever thinking that leaving was a viable option for us.

I rarely saw my mother stand up for herself, and yet she was strong.

There was no safe way out for my mother.

There were no safety nets to catch her, and the very real risk of having her children removed if she exposed the truth of the violence happening inside the home.

Leaving meant no home, no money and—of greater consequence—the deep shame that threatened to attach itself to a family in a small country town.

This shame came with invisible tendrils that perhaps my mother believed would threaten to steal any hope of a future.

There was a stigma if your family was viewed as dysfunctional.

A stigma that limited opportunities.

Opportunities to escape.

After I had left home, in spite of rationally understanding the reasons my mother stayed with our father, I am almost ashamed to admit that a deep, silent resentment began to emerge. A resentment that I didn't know I carried.

It was a simmering, quiet anger that would surface in unrecognisable ways.

I would find myself feeling frustrated with her for no apparent reason. I was suddenly embarrassed about her weight, even though I knew it was a consequence of comfort-eating for most of her life.

Any sign of weakness I saw in her seemed to frustrate me.

I wanted to scream at my mother to stand up and count in the world.

I despised the unworthiness that seemed to plague her, dimming her gifts and smothering her purpose.

Her life had been totally derailed by domestic violence.

A conundrum of mixed emotions resided deep within me and I was unsure how to reconcile such competing feelings of both deep love and resentment.

I had chosen long ago to cling to my mother's love like a drowning child might cling to her rescuer in a raging torrent of water.

I may not have drowned, but sadly, in spite of my great love and respect for my mother, I came out of the water drenched, cold and afraid.

ROGUE WAVES

"*For I have placed the sand as a boundary for the sea. Though the waves toss, yet they cannot prevail; Though they roar, yet they cannot cross over it.*"
Jeremiah 5:22 (NASB)

My childhood fears were being awoken with each new life challenge that arrived, but I was determined to bury them beneath the shiny veneer of my new married life. At times, I felt like that young girl in the surf again, struggling to make her way through the waves, beyond the break, where life would be calm again. Only this time, I was swimming alone, with no uncle's hand to hold, and at the mercy of the waves rolling toward me. It was becoming painfully obvious that I had to learn to swim by myself.

No one was coming to save me.

I had to find my own way back to the shore.

My husband is a surfer. Apparently, when a huge wave has knocked you off your board it is best to stop resisting and roll with the wave until it has lost its power. Whilst I have never surfed, his description of being held down in the impact zone sounded eerily like the anxiety that was holding me down. Whilst the child in me was floundering in the water at the mercy of the waves, I knew instinctively I had to find a resilience based on my adult self.

Postnatal depression, however, was a formidable enemy. I had to find the courage to swim beyond those waves, where I could float on my back for a while and work out what I needed to do. I needed time to just lie on my back, with my arms outstretched, surrendering to the rise and fall of the waves.

Surrendering.

A frightening concept.

To surrender the fight was not an option for me as a young girl as that would have left my mother defenceless.

The all-consuming darkness of postnatal depression, however, would ironically become an unexpected gift on my path to healing. A gift that would finally force this warrior child to raise her white flag, lay down her weapons and understand that true surrender was the only way forward.

The journey of surrender, however, is not a road that should be travelled alone.

It is at this point I am going to speak with full and open transparency about the most important key to my own personal healing.

That key has been my faith in God.

If you have found the courage to be vulnerable and return to the battlefield of your childhood, do not return alone. Gather some troops around you.

Most importantly, find a captain you can trust.

My captain, was Jesus.

I returned to my childhood memories fully equipped, with Jesus at the helm, and troops who were ready for battle. Troops who knew the power of prayer.

Be brave, stand and stare directly at every single messed-up moment of your childhood.

Jesus loves turning mess into miracles.

I LOVED the vulnerability of my children when they were young.

A vulnerability I didn't seem to have. I mean, who wants to stand open and unprotected, without armour in an unsafe world.

They however, were vulnerable with both their physicality as well as their emotional selves. My boys always seemed eager to connect with others with raw honesty and transparency. They weren't afraid of the world.

The child who grows up keeping the peace at all costs in order to stay safe, however, becomes an adult who is reticent to have an opinion contrary to others, or to express how they really feel. Forcing one's feelings down is exhausting. If left unchecked, it will eventually lead to bitterness and resentment. The "peace at all costs" child may also become the eternal people pleaser, over-generously pouring themselves into others, to keep them happy. An unsustainable position, really.

I recall sitting as a young mother, watching with envy the free abandonment with which my young sons would swim in our backyard pool. Diving beneath the surface, at one with the water, as they enjoyed its cool fluidity for hours on end. The best part was when they would pop up from under the water and smile at me, with droplets of water running down their delighted faces.

My fear of being vulnerable has been challenged time and again over the years and I am slowly but reluctantly learning that it's unavoidable if we want to remain authentic with ourselves and the people around us. Surely as we age, we get to rest on our laurels a little, so to speak? Seemingly, that's not the case in my life. Even more recently, when an injury to my foot meant I could no longer walk for exercise, my willingness to be vulnerable was tested yet again. Consequently, I found myself tentatively climbing down the stairs of our local pool at the suggestion of my physiotherapist. I had never really dwelled on the reasons why I felt uncomfortable with my head submerged in water, other than the fact it probably was another leftover childhood need to stay in control.

Learning how to swim properly was not a high priority in the country, and swimming lessons generally consisted of being hurled into the deep end of the fifty-metre Olympic swimming pool, surrounded by hordes of other kids flailing around, as you dog paddled frantically back to the edge.

Therefore, it was a dog paddling expert climbing down those pool stairs, grumbling about how cold the water was.

As I gazed down the length of the pool lane that seemed to stretch out forever before me, I knew instinctively it was finally time to let go and trust myself, not only to the water but more fully to the world around me. And here's the thing.

Healing is not static.

Wholeness gently unfolds, as we lean in.

I looked around, envious of the other swimmers who seemed so peaceful, their effortless strokes propelling them down the pool, and again I felt like an impostor. But I had recognised and long overcome those feelings of not belonging, and I pulled my goggles firmly into place, inhaled deeply, and lowered my face into the cold water. I was tentative, and yet with every clumsy stroke a new-found freedom began to wash over me.

It seemed like, with each stroke, I was reclaiming the final parts of myself that had been lost.

I reached the other end of the pool, and came up gasping for air and yet smiling broadly, just as my children had, all those years earlier, in our backyard pool.

THE LETTER

"*The weak can never forgive. Forgiveness is the attribute of the strong.*" Mahatma Ghandi

I wrote the letter late one night.

I'm not sure if I really meant it at the time, but I was a new mother and I had an overwhelming desire to find wholeness in myself, for the sake of my husband and children. I wanted to be the best mother I could be. I had seen the power of forgiveness at work in the generations of women that had gone before me and I instinctively knew it was what I needed to do. It wasn't some grand gesture on my part, just a yearning to finally rise above my past, so it could no longer define me.

I lifted my pen to write and there was no sentimental gush of words that flowed effortlessly onto the page.

In fact, initially, nothing flowed at all.

Only anger, followed closely by the usual suspects of shame and fear.

I wasn't entirely sure the old man even deserved my

forgiveness. But, in spite of my feelings, I began to write.

Dear Dad

I am writing to let you know that I forgive you.

I now realise you were doing the best you could at the time and you had no help to overcome your addiction to alcohol.

I don't need you to write back to me, and I don't want this letter to bring up the past and make you feel guilt or shame.

I just want you to know that you are forgiven.

I release all bitterness toward you.

I love you.

Your daughter,

Susan x

I read over what I had written, and was surprised at what had poured onto the page. I didn't feel any self-righteous feelings of superiority.

I simply made a choice, to forgive my father.

It was some time after I had written the letter, that I noticed a change within me. It was subtle at first, hardly recognisable.

This final act of forgiveness seemed to confront the pain of my childhood and release its hold upon my life.

Releasing my father had in fact released me.

Dad never spoke of the letter.

An unspoken forgiveness settled into our relationship.

I saw it in subtle ways at first, when we spoke, and the way he loved my children as a grandfather.

As I watched him interact with my children in later years, as a healed and whole man, I saw the love that was supposed to have been mine, poured out upon them.

It was like his love had missed an entire generation.

My father was finally forced to overcome his dependency on alcohol following the loss of his job as a barman, which removed him from the temptation found in his everyday working environment. The miracle I had been praying for most of my childhood, turned up at the end of my final year of school.

I was free to go to university, unchained from the burden of keeping my mother safe.

The dance for me, was finally over.

How incredibly sad that he had been lost in the shadow of addiction for fifteen years of his short life. It should have come as no surprise that his hard drinking and smoking would take a toll on his health.

And so it was that he died suddenly and unexpectedly from a stroke at seventy-two years of age.

The day I heard the news from my sister, I cried inconsolably.

It was not with the normal grief of a daughter losing a father.

It was grief for the father I so desperately wanted and yet never had.

At least I had made peace with him.

Following my father's death, my mother found the letter I had written some years earlier—in his wallet, in the top drawer of his bedside table.

It was folded, and the weathered edges of the notepaper indicated it had been well read.

I do not really know whether my father was able to find forgiveness for himself, but the letter had undoubtedly unlocked healing and renewal in my own life.

I hope my father found some peace in his later years.

Enough joy had already been stolen, from both of us.

A NEW DANCE

"*There is nothing like returning to a place that remains unchanged to find the ways in which you yourself have altered.*" Nelson Mandela

There is a strange melancholic freedom about returning to your home town after both your parents have moved beyond this physical world. A sentimental journey to look honestly and squarely at both the pain and joy that was woven through the fabric of your childhood.

To wander the same streets, be accosted by the familiar smell of the eucalyptus trees. To hear the raucous cry of the cockatoos as they swoop, and trace the bends of the river.

To laugh, to cry and to remember.

A therapeutic journey.

A final reckoning.

As I strolled up the hill from my old home, retracing the steps I used to walk to school as a young girl, I found myself standing at the front fence of the white Cape Cod house where Anne lived. The garden was a little neglected, with weeds amidst the shrubs in the front garden beds. The huge pine tree still remained, dominating the front garden like a monument to the years that had passed. I walked tentatively down the gravel driveway, my confidence waning a little with each step, like I had suddenly left my adult self at the front gate and I was that young schoolgirl once again. From a distance, I could see an elderly woman sitting on the front veranda, warming herself in the winter sun. I was surprised by the familiar rush of childhood unworthiness that had tried to usurp the grown-up me walking down that driveway.

I lifted my head and stood up straighter, in an effort to rebuke that long-outdated melody. As I came closer, I realised it was Anne's' mum. I approached slowly so as not startle her, in case she didn't recognise me.

"Hello," I said.

She looked curiously at my face, and you could see her pondering, trying to reach back into her memory and find the right connections.

The young skinny girl from primary school who chased hockey balls alongside her daughter was very different to the middle-aged woman standing in her front garden now.

"It's Suzy, Anne's friend from primary school," I gently announced.

"Oh, my goodness. Hello, Suzy. I'm so sorry I didn't recognise you at first."

Her warm tone had not disappeared, though the years had aged her physical frame. She looked slim and healthy, and a peace was lightly resting on her face as she sat soaking up the warm winter sun.

I found myself reflecting on the contrast between this woman, who appeared to have aged peacefully, and my mother's later years, spent battling cancer. My mother had lived just two years beyond my father. Her life had been totally devoted to her family, nursing her own mother to the ripe old age of ninety-eight. When she became ill herself, it was unexpected and seemed such an unjust outcome for such a generous, kind woman.

My faith however assures me there is more after this life.

I have had to accept and find peace in the fact that the rewards of my mother's sacrificial life will live on and be enjoyed by the generations that will follow.

A legacy of love that can never be erased.

Anne's mother and I exchanged polite conversation about my life and hers. The conversation soon turned to Anne and her wonderful contribution to the field of medicine and cancer. As we sat together, in the garden, I was aware of a new-found confidence in myself. We talked about the fence between the school and their home and our lunchtime escapades in search of lime cordial, and she laughed.

I could see that the fence had long been repaired with no trace of its former self remaining. The old timber posts had been torn down and rebuilt, much the same way my life had been rebuilt. And yet as the conversation returned to Anne and her incredible career achievements, a surprising remnant of unworthiness rose up again. I knew instinctively what I needed to do to put this beast to rest once and for all.

Reconnect with Anne.

Some time passed after my visit to my home town, and yet still the nagging thought persisted about making contact with Anne. Perhaps she would not even remember the skinny redhead from primary school. I summoned up the courage to search out her location and contact details.

As I crafted an email to my childhood friend, Anne's professional credentials of Associate Professor screamed at me.

This time, however, I was not so quick to dance to that old childhood melody. My finger went straight to the send button, and, after a deep breath, I hit the key firmly. The reply was swifter than I had expected, and was sitting in my inbox after only a few days. Anne was polite and thanked me for visiting her Mum, and said she would be happy to meet for a coffee. As I sat reading her reply, I realised it was done.

Whether we met in the future or not, it would not be to validate my worthiness, but rather, to simply enjoy a coffee with an old friend.

My sentimental wander back through the country

town I grew up in was always going to end on the banks of the Macquarie River.

To just sit and remember.

I was surprised to see the old, thick, gnarled log we played on as children still there, reaching awkwardly out into the middle of the river. I crawled tentatively along to the furthest reach of that log and straddled its wide girth with my legs. I sat and reflected upon my life as a young girl, as I watched the river swirling its own unique path around that log.

I could almost hear the sound of family voices echoing from the surrounding bush, smell burnt sausages and hear stones skipping across the water from family barbecues on those familiar riverbanks.

The sound of the trickling water calmed this dancing daughter once again, and in the solitude, I realised this river held sacred memories of days gone by and precious family members both loved and lost.

The irony of life was that this log had remained fixed and immovable, whilst the river had swirled and eddied around its roots for so many years in my absence.

I had been on my own journey, while this river had faithfully continued to flow.

A brave journey, where I had learned so much.

I had learned that while childhood wounds are painful, once healed, they can leave precious gifts behind.

Gifts for others.

Gifts like empathy, forgiveness, unconditional love and grace.

This dancing daughter had bravely silenced the destructive, discordant childhood melody that had been left playing in the background of her life.

She had courageously choreographed a new dance.

A dance of forgiveness, courage and faith.

~

 "He heals the wounds of every shattered heart." Psalm 147:3 (TPT)

Susan's parents on their wedding day.

Susan's father (L) photographed during World War II.

PHOTOGRAPHS

Susan's family home in Dubbo, New South Wales, with their car parked out the front.

A family Easter celebration in Dubbo.
Susan is second from left in front row.

Seaside holidays, with Uncle Rex at left.

Susan with her beloved dog, Sammy - who was always on the move!

PHOTOGRAPHS

Susan's grandparents, whom she called Mardi and Pardi.

Susan's grandmother, Mardi (front left), mourning the death of her own father.

PHOTOGRAPHS

Susan's father working as a bar tender.

Susan's thirteenth birthday — teenage bliss!

PHOTOGRAPHS

Susan's father demonstrating waltz steps.

A new dance — Susan's wedding day.

ABOUT THE AUTHOR

Susan Lambert is a teacher who lives with her husband in a small Australian coastal community near the Pacific Ocean. Her greatest fulfilment has been found in being the mother of two grown up sons. *Dancing Daughter* is her first book.

susanlambert.com.au

DOMESTIC AND FAMILY VIOLENCE
SUPPORT SERVICES, AUSTRALIA

The National Sexual Assault, Family & Domestic Violence Counselling Line (free and confidential advice 24/7) – 1800 RESPECT, 1800 737 732.

Lifeline can connect you with a crisis service in your state – 131 114.

Police or Ambulance – dial 000 in an emergency.

Kids Help Line – 1800 551 800, kidshelp.com.au.

Australian Childhood Foundation – 1800 381 581, childhood.org.au.

Blue Knot Foundation (Adults Surviving Child Abuse) – 1300 657 380, asca.org.au.

www.ingramcontent.com/pod-product-compliance
Lightning Source LLC
Chambersburg PA
CBHW032041290426
44110CB00012B/901